I0824137

Fresh Mercies Every Day

Cultivate a Life of Trusting God, Following Him Daily, and Learning to Flourish

JENNIE LUSKO

Fresh Mercies Every Day

Published by Thomas Nelson, 501 Nelson Place, Nashville, TN 37214, USA. Thomas Nelson is a registered trademark of HarperCollins Christian Publishing, Inc.

Thomas Nelson titles may be purchased in bulk for educational, business, fundraising, or sales promotional use. For information, please email SpecialMarkets@ThomasNelson.com.

ISBN 978-1-4002-5234-3 (HC)
ISBN 978-1-4002-5231-2 (audiobook)
ISBN 978-1-4002-5230-5 (eBook)

HarperCollins Publishers, Macken House, 39/40 Mayor Street Upper, Dublin 1, D01 C9W8, Ireland
(https://www.harpercollins.com)

Art direction: Tiffany Forrester
Cover design: Elisha Gregory
Cover lettering: Nat Hogle
Interior design: Kristina Juodenas
Interior lettering: Jennie Lusko
Photography: Jennifer Dillon
Additional photography: Latisha Lyn Photography (page 194)

Printed in India

25 26 27 28 29 REP 10 9 8 7 6 5 4 3 2 1

Alivia Sky,

Lenya Avery,

Daisy Grace,

Clover Dawn:

Each of you is stunning. You shine so bright and light up my life.

You are my favorites, and God has beautiful, unique plans for each of you.

Soon and very soon, Len Len.

And to every lovely lady in my life—past, present, and future—who has inspired, influenced, or impacted my life in such a variety of ways, thank you.

CONTENTS

FRESH MERCY #2:
FOLLOWING GOD EVERY SINGLE DAY

FRESH MERCY #3:
TRUSTING GOD IN EVERYTHING

FRESH MERCY #4: BECOMING MORE LIKE JESUS

FRESH MERCY #5: BELIEVING GOD WHEN IT DOESN'T MAKE SENSE

GOOD MORNING, LORD

Through the LORD's mercies we are not consumed,
Because His compassions fail not.
They are new every morning;
Great is Your faithfulness.
"The LORD is my portion," says my soul,
"Therefore I hope in Him!"
The LORD is good to those who wait for Him,
To the soul who seeks Him.

LAMENTATIONS 3:22–25

EVER SINCE I WAS SIXTEEN, I have started many of my journal entries with *Good morning, Lord* (usually with a heart drawn next to it). There's a feeling of a fresh start in this prayer. And looking back at my many (maybe *too* many) journal entries, there was a sweetness to these words. No matter what was happening in my life, there was still a newness, a freshness, and a sense of anticipation for all that God held for me in the day ahead.

My heart in these pages is that you would be encouraged to start your day (whether you're an early bird or a night owl) with the wondrous grace of God. Depending fully on His love, His mercy, and His view of you, with the knowledge that trusting Him in the little things will create the flourishing life you desire.

Fresh Mercies Every Day is a call to see our lives the way God does and to recognize the tiny moments as huge opportunities for God to show up in significant ways.

The Lord's mercies, compassion, and love are fresh every day. He alone is faithful. And this truth leads us to say to ourselves, "The LORD is my portion. . . . Therefore I hope in Him!" (Lamentations 3:24). It causes us to pause. To wait *for* Him and *on* Him so we can see His goodness firsthand.

I also want to highlight the beautiful photography and creativity of my friend Jenn Dillon. She has been in my life for nearly two decades, and she has been a source of joy, strength, and depth to me and to all who know her. Years ago she decided to design and create a garden full of the most gorgeous flowers. It has been part of the healing and strengthening in her own story, and it symbolizes her daily trust in the Lord. Her photography fills these pages, and she captures the beauty of these blooms with such a creative eye! My prayer is that these photos will inspire creativity in your own life, helping you to notice the beauty God has for you in everything you see, experience, and hold. In your pain, in your prosperity, He is right there with you, and there is beauty in every single day.

THERE IS BEAUTY IN EVERY SINGLE DAY.

Lord Jesus, draw my sister into Your love today. I pray that she would see Your fresh mercies as Your invitation—in this very moment—to see You in a new light. To see Your love as the banner over her heart, mind, life, and impact. You have deep flourishing for her today. Amen.

SO, WHAT'S MERCY AGAIN?

If we're leaning into God's fresh mercies every day, let's have a brief refresher about what mercy actually is. I have always confused grace and mercy, so let's start with grace (which is always a good place to start). God's grace is stunning. It's found in the blessings He gives us that we don't deserve, like salvation and kindness. ("For by grace you have been saved through faith, and that not of ourselves; it is the gift of God, not of works, lest anyone should boast" [Ephesians 2:8–9].)

Mercy, on the other hand? It is *not* being given what we *do* deserve. Wait—what? This can seem a little harsh. What *do* we deserve? Because our sin separates us from God, there is a divide between us and God that we could never bridge on our own. Our sin makes us stuck. But because of Jesus, we now have a way back to God when before there was no way. Jesus took what we deserved for our sin, which was punishment and death. That's what we actually deserved—it was the penalty for sin. But thanks be to God for such great salvation! Because of Jesus, we have life, we have freedom, we have hope, we have purpose, and we have everything we need for life and godliness! *Mercy!* This is what it looks like to not receive what we do deserve.

So, if His mercies are new each morning, it's actually a beautiful reminder of our salvation. Of what we *would* have if it weren't for Jesus. And because of Him—His life and His sacrifice—we get to surrender our lives to Him and walk in this newness of life. We get fresh mercies today. We get to wake up and walk in His love in a fresh way. This will change the way we live. This will change everything!

Love, Jennie

Fresh Mercy #1

GROWING IN DEEPER INTIMACY WITH GOD

WHAT ABOUT MY NEEDS?

And my God shall supply all your need according to His riches in glory by Christ Jesus. Now to our God and Father be glory forever and ever. Amen.

PHILIPPIANS 4:19–20

Lord, thank You that I don't have to be my own strength and shield, and that I don't have to find them on my own. You haven't left me alone—but not only that, You're with me now. And You're not only with me; You're protecting me and giving me the strength to walk forward. O, Christ, be the center of my life. Be the place where I lift my eyes; help me focus my attention on You. Amen.

I recently learned in counseling that what I need most from my husband, Levi, is connection and closeness. When we discovered this, it connected some major dots for me and made sense of past conflict in our relationship. I often expect Levi to automatically know what I need. I expect him to draw me close and give me the warmth, attention, care, and security that I crave. There are certainly ways in which he can and *does* offer this to me. However, I can also go about getting my needs met in the wrong way. Specifically, I can be tempted to expect from Levi what I should expect only from Jesus.

When I'm receiving from Jesus, He is meeting the deep needs of my heart. He is giving me what only He can give: validation, worth, attention, unconditional love, joy, and true closeness. And the beauty of this affects my relationships—my marriage, friendships, parenting, and every other encounter—because I can then engage with others as a person who is already secure and affirmed. When I am secure in Christ, I can bring my best self to others, and as a result, I'm able to share from the overflow that happens when Jesus truly meets my deepest needs.

WHEN I AM SECURE IN CHRIST, I CAN BRING MY BEST SELF TO OTHERS.

I feel such a difference when I look to Jesus, allowing Him to meet me where I am. When

I make room for Him to remain at the center of my life, I am able to love myself and others better.

Each one of us has longings that need to be not only met but also fully satisfied. Like I mentioned earlier, mine are connection and closeness. Maybe you need safety and security. Whatever the deepest needs of your heart may be, I encourage you to make time and space to be with Jesus, allowing Him to meet you, heal you, and fill you. Then, let that time with Him fuel your connection with others.

INVITING THE LORD'S PRESENCE INTO THIS MOMENT

Your Father knows you, inside and out. He is the One who knit you together in your mother's womb, the One who knows exactly what you need in this moment. Spend some time with Him now, asking Him to open up your heart and mind, and welcome God to show you what you need. How has He shown you His nearness? What desires and thoughts might be hindering Him from filling you to overflowing? Lay them at His feet. Breathe. Surrender. Rest in His perfect love for you.

STANDING FIRM

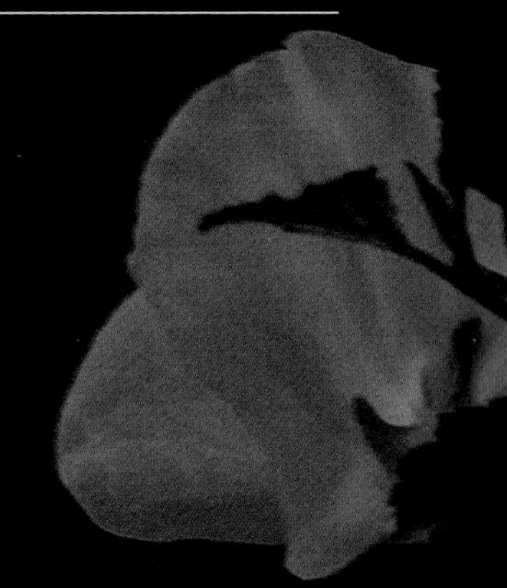

I waited patiently for the LORD;
And He inclined to me,
And heard my cry.
He also brought me up out of a horrible pit,
Out of the miry clay;
And set my feet upon a rock,
And established my steps.
He has put a new song in my mouth—
Praise to our God.

PSALM 40:1–3

God, I want You to change me. I want to be transformed to be more like You. Give me the discipline to encounter You in Your Word. Let Your Word live in me. Help me to stand firm in You so that I can sing a new song of praise to You. Amen.

LET'S TALK ABOUT TURNING FORTY. If you aren't forty currently, you're either heading toward it or you're looking back at it in the rearview mirror. Wherever you are on the getting-older-and-even-more-beautiful spectrum, it's worth considering what it means to age well and how to live *life* well.

Before I entered my forties, I had heard that turning forty was a pivotal and powerful transition for many of my friends. After their fortieth birthdays, they felt more comfortable in their skin, found a greater joy and strength in life, became more fit, and experienced many other awesome things—all of which made me look forward to turning forty myself. Hearing this, I wanted to go into my forties with a strong stance and be just a little more "ready on my toes" for whatever revelation or season God had for me next. I wanted to surrender to the Lord in a fresh way, asking Him to go before me, change me, and develop me. So I made the decision to fast for forty days. And I ran a half-marathon. (You know, the kinds of things it seems like you're supposed to do when you become a forty-year-old.)

Around this time, my husband preached a message about the life of our church, Fresh Life, encouraging us to memorize Scripture, and reminding us what it could do for our hearts, our minds, and our lives. So I took him up on it, and all I can say is that *it was life-changing.* I ended up finding great fortitude at forty, especially in memorizing this stunning psalm, Psalm 40.

Can you hear how the word *fort* is nestled in the word *forty*? (I do. Because I'm weird with words like that.) I have found such strength and joy in growing older in the Lord. There is always *more* with Him. More grace, more peace, more wisdom, more joy, more life—all the more there is! And my prayer for you is that as you age, you would find greater depth and strength in God—your Creator, your King, and your Prince of Peace.

Just as my life was revitalized by memorizing this psalm, I encourage you to also consider memorizing a passage of Scripture that means a lot to you. Start small, and watch to see what God will do! In Psalm 40 the psalmist announced that God "set my feet upon a rock, and established my steps" (v. 2). And I can testify that this is exactly what He does when we allow His Word to dwell in our hearts and minds and on our lips—as we lean on Him with everything in us.

INVITING THE LORD'S PRESENCE INTO THIS MOMENT

Lord, You are the One who lifted me out of the pit and set my feet on a rock. God, I want to live my life standing on You, my Rock, and in Your Word and Truth. Show me what passage of Scripture You are inviting me to internalize by keeping it in my heart and mind. Amen.

Think of a scripture that has been a theme of your life or a cry of your heart. How has God ministered to you through His Word in this passage? Take a moment and consider His Word, then write down some options that come to your mind. Remember, start small and see what God will do.

WHEN I AM AFRAID

When you lie down, you will not be afraid;
Yes, you will lie down and your sleep will be sweet.
Do not be afraid of sudden terror,
Nor of trouble from the wicked when it comes;
For the LORD will be your confidence,
And will keep your foot from being caught.

PROVERBS 3:24–26

Father, when I have a sleepless night, would You help me remember to turn my sleepy eyes and heart toward You? Whether I'm up with a child, my spouse, a pet, or my own anxieties and worries, may I run to You first for strength, for peace, or for guidance. Show me whom You might want me to pray for or how I might need to surrender something—or someone—to Your capable hands. Thank You, Lord.

ONE NIGHT WHEN OUR GIRLS were young and Levi was out of town, our oldest daughter, Livie, was in bed with me. We had read and prayed together, and she was sleeping soundly. I was about to doze off when I heard Clover, our youngest, crying.

Slipping out of bed and walking to Clover's room, I peered into her crib. Covered by her blankets from head to toe, she'd somehow gotten tangled up in them and was both stuck and scared. I pulled her out and snuggled her to comfort her, then I put her back down and carefully swaddled her back up into the proper baby-burrito situation.

I snuck back into bed with Livie, and I'd been asleep for about an hour when I heard Clover cry again. Once more, I found she had wriggled out of her swaddle and was again stuck in her blankets. After comforting her and rocking her back to sleep, I laid her on the mattress and swaddled her back up, a little tighter this time.

By the time I finally got back in my own bed, it was well after one in the morning, and I couldn't sleep. After lying motionless for a while and telling myself to *Just go to sleep, woman!* I sat up and switched on my bedside light. I don't know if I was overly tired, shaken by Clover's restlessness, or just bothered by the darkness, but I felt uneasy.

I reached for my phone and turned on some Hillsong worship music. I read the lyrics to a hymn we'd sung in church about God being seated on a throne in heaven. I read my Bible out loud: "Whenever I am afraid, I will trust in You. In God (I will praise His word), in God I have put my trust" (Psalm 56:3–4). I was also comforted by God's assurance in Proverbs: "When you lie down, you will not be afraid" (Proverbs 3:24). Finally, comforted by God's nearness, I lay down and went back to sleep.

I OFFERED MY SLEEPLESSNESS TO GOD AND LET HIM MINISTER TO ME.

There have been plenty of nights when I've tossed and turned and worried. But on nights like this one, I offered my sleeplessness to God and let Him minister to me. A much better option that I somehow tend to forget more often than I'd like to admit.

INVITING THE LORD'S PRESENCE INTO THIS MOMENT

If you are ever up at night with worry or anxiety over the things you can't control, you are not alone. When we offer what weighs on our hearts and minds to God, He is so kind to meet us. Next time this happens to you, spend some time acknowledging that you are indeed carrying things you weren't meant to carry. Name them. Then give them to God one by one. He is the only One who can truly hold your cares and comfort you when you are afraid. Let Him. Be still in His presence, and let His love steady your soul.

A GLEAM IN HIS EYE

Therefore we do not lose heart. Even though our outward man is perishing, yet the inward man is being renewed day by day. For our light affliction, which is but for a moment, is working for us a far more exceeding and eternal weight of glory, while we do not look at the things which are seen, but at the things which are not seen. For the things which are seen are temporary, but the things which are not seen are eternal.

2 CORINTHIANS 4:16–18

Lord God, thank You for seeing me. And not only that, thank You for showing me that You know me, because You designed me. You have been so faithful to show me Your presence in small ways and in huge ways. Give me the eyes to recognize these sweet moments today, especially the gleam in Your eye when You look at Your precious kids. I love You.

"I know you!"

I was checking out at T.J.Maxx when the cashier recognized me from church. "I know you!" she gushed. "It's great to see you!" This young woman went on to tell me how she was a part of our church, Fresh Life, and how her life had been radically changed by God. We continued to chat for a bit about small groups and being on a team, and we both marveled at how good God is.

As I walked back to my car, I thought about an experience that Levi and I had had in that *same* store six years earlier. At that time, we were living in Dana Point, California, and were just visiting Kalispell, Montana. We'd stopped in to T.J.Maxx and asked an employee if she knew of a church in the area that she would recommend. Sadly, she couldn't, explaining, "I go to a small church here, but I wouldn't tell anybody to go there." Her answer broke my heart.

Our encounter that afternoon seemed small, but I also think it was significant. I found it so beautiful that, six years later, a different young woman recognized me from church and she was growing and thriving at Fresh Life, right in Kalispell. It was in this brief moment that God reminded me of who He is, what He's done, and what He *is still doing*. It felt like what some people call a "God wink" or a "God moment." And it reminded me of the way my Grandpa Dave would mischievously wink when he teased or had fun with one of us grandkids.

KEEP YOUR EYES OPEN FOR THESE GOD WINKS.

Have you ever had a sweet moment like this, when God seems to be winking, letting you know, *I've done this. I'm doing it. I've got it. Just you watch!*? Keep your eyes open for these God winks. And imagine Him laughing and smiling as He sends them your way. When you recognize that God is not only at work in the world but that He's at work in *your* world, let it lift your heart, mind, and soul.

INVITING THE LORD'S PRESENCE INTO THIS MOMENT

More often than not we forget to pause to notice what God is doing around us. Take a moment to look back at the last few days. Think about the small ways God has shown Himself to you. Think of the times He used you to encourage someone. Maybe it was super small. (Those can be the hardest to remember.) Write a few of these down. Ask God to help you be more aware of His presence in the seemingly small moments today. Take note to help your future self remember more easily.

EXCITED TO ENCOUNTER HIS WORD

I rejoice at Your word
As one who finds great treasure.
I hate and abhor lying,
But I love Your law.
Seven times a day I praise You,
Because of Your righteous judgments.
Great peace have those who love Your law,
And nothing causes them to stumble.

PSALM 119:162–165

God, I know You're here to meet with me. Who am I that the God of all creation would want to spend time with me? Forgive me for being the one who so often breaks my appointment with You! I do hunger and thirst for more of You, but my body doesn't usually get the memo, and it loves sleep and comfort so much. O Lord, thank You for the sweet little reminders from Your Word. Your Word strengthens me, no matter what I'm facing. Amen.

SOMETIMES WE HAVE BEAUTIFUL, SPACIOUS amounts of time to spend with God, and other times it's like we're using a rubber spatula to scrape out whatever we can get. I remember when our kids were younger and it was a real challenge to find the time I wanted and needed to be with the Lord. And now that I'm older, it still can be a struggle, just in different ways.

One day, when the kids were little, I planned to get up early, shower, and have my Bible and tea time—all before the girls woke up. I think I even planned to get a workout in. A girl can dream! Well, thirty minutes before my alarm was set to go off, Liv woke up sick and was throwing up. After caring for her, I showered, and by the time I got out, Lenya was awake and ready to get out of bed. It was a travel day, and I was scrambling to get us all ready to go to the airport.

There was finally a brief moment of quiet, so I snuck away to my room and began to read Psalm 27. I'd just started the chapter when Lenya ran in and needed something. But look at how good God is, to speak so sweetly and clearly in the few moments I did have. I had actually only made it through the first verse, but on that day, when I was dreading what was ahead—especially traveling with a sick child—God met me: "The LORD is my light and my salvation; whom shall I fear? The LORD is the strength of my life; of whom shall I be afraid?" (v. 1).

It felt so sweet that, in the midst of my tiredness, and so much sickness, the Lord reminded me how He is the defense of my life. It makes me think of the supplements that promise to be a healthy defense against illness and disease. No matter what I'm facing—lack of sleep, vomiting children, not getting done what I wanted to do—God is my defense. He is my light and my salvation. What am I so afraid of?

HE IS MY LIGHT AND MY SALVATION.

INVITING THE LORD'S PRESENCE INTO THIS MOMENT

Sometimes we long to hear God speak to us through His Word, but actually settling in to be still and focus can be the most challenging thing. Recently, my husband preached a message on prayer, and he asked us to think of our favorite celebrity or musical artist. If that person were to enter our living room, we would probably pee a little (his words, ha-ha), but then we would focus on our guest, get off our phones, limit distractions, and lean in. Dear heart, this is your moment. The God of the universe—the King of kings and the Lord of lords—is not only stopping by to see you; He *wants* to speak to you, listen to you, and give you everything you actually need! Open His Word today, and ask Him to open your eyes to see the glorious truths recorded there. Even if it's one verse, reflect on what God is saying to you today and open your life to Him in a fresh way.

A GUT FEELING

"I am the vine, you are the branches. He who abides in Me, and I in him, bears much fruit; for without Me you can do nothing. . . . If you abide in Me, and My words abide in you, you will ask what you desire, and it shall be done for you."

JOHN 15:5, 7

Lord Jesus, I need You every hour. Every moment. Every minute. Thank You for the way You allow struggles, situations, or even that feeling in the pit of my stomach, to draw me closer to You and deeper in relationship with You. Thank You, God.

A while back, Levi and I had the opportunity to travel and do ministry together in California. We had the privilege of being part of a night of ministry and worship with the incarcerated men at San Quentin Rehabilitation Center. Before my husband preached at this event, we spent a little time with the group of people who were serving that night, and a few people in the circle took the opportunity to share what was on their hearts.

Like I do in most impromptu moments like this, I wondered if I should even share, but then I took a deep breath and decided to tell the group, "Every day I wake up with a feeling deep in the pit of my stomach about the day ahead." I went on, "I feel like, even if I have planned out the day, I really have no idea what to expect, what to do, or how to finish what is on my schedule."

I also wanted to share with them that this odd feeling was part of my daily walk with God. "It's such a strange feeling to wake up like that," I continued, "and then get to surrender it all to the Lord and say, 'God, I need You! I can't face this day, or any of its opportunities, decisions, and interactions, without You. If You don't go with me and fill me with Your love and Your power, I can't go. I can't do this without You! And I don't want to.'"

Have you felt that anxious rumbling deep down? That fine line between excitement and anxiety? Various studies have demonstrated that there's a remarkable connection between our guts and our brains, and one of the things they've discovered is that anxious feelings and excited feelings are so similar they register almost the same in the brain and nervous system.

Levi has preached that when we feel nervous about something, the way we talk about it matters. He has said that if we shift our thinking from *fear* to naming something we are excited about, we can reframe that thing in our minds. This has helped me so much whenever I enter a new day and am facing things that scare me or make me nervous.

IF WE SHIFT OUR THINKING FROM FEAR TO NAMING SOMETHING WE ARE EXCITED ABOUT, WE CAN REFRAME THAT THING IN OUR MINDS.

Today I've actually become thankful for that feeling in the pit of my stomach when I look toward the day ahead. It focuses my attention on Jesus and puts Him back in the center of my heart and my life where He belongs, and it points me back to the moment when He reminded His first disciples that without Him, they could do nothing (John 15:5).

INVITING THE LORD'S PRESENCE INTO THIS MOMENT

Do you ever experience that rumbling in the pit of your stomach, reminding you that you need God to help you do whatever lies before you in this day? Jesus reminds us that without Him, we can do nothing. Take a moment and talk to God about the areas of your life in which you need to allow the Vine to do what only He can do. Surrender to the work of your Father, and let His love flow in and through you as you tell Him how desperate you are for Him.

THE ONE THING

And Jesus answered and said to her, "Martha, Martha, you are worried and troubled about many things. But one thing is needed, and Mary has chosen that good part, which will not be taken away from her."

LUKE 10:41–42

Lord, whatever comes my way today, help me to see the beauty of focusing on You. I desire the one thing that Mary found at Your feet, and in Your presence. Help me to simplify my soul and clean out the clutter in my mind and heart. I wait on You now, my Lord and my King and my Friend. Amen.

Most days I am an actual struggle bus.

Even when I start my day in the Word and in prayer and stillness, there comes a point when I am faced with the real struggles and tiny decisions of the day. These little choices make a huge impact, and I find myself easily doubting myself, then scrambling, and then allowing myself to get flustered, which generally leads to me being late. I wish I could blame homeschooling, or our kids, or anything else, but, to be honest, *it comes down to me* and my struggle to prepare and plan and just be focused.

A few weeks ago, knowing I'd be rushing from one thing to the next throughout the day, I got really clever with packing my bags. I put the books I needed in one bag, and I dropped the clothes I'd need in another bag. I even used a cute little tote for my wallet, keys, ChapStick, hand lotion, and readers (I need them more and more these days!). With this multitude of bags strapped to my body, I rushed to hop in the Jeep and share a ride to church with Levi. But the moment I stuffed myself in the passenger seat, I realized I couldn't find my phone. After rifling through all the bags, I ran inside and searched everywhere. Knowing that Levi needed to get going, I resolved to make it one day without it.

Oh, man. Not having my phone with me for a whole day? *Breathe, Jennie, just breathe.*

Luke told the story of this woman—who was for sure more organized than me, but who very *much* like me got caught up in the busyness of the day—and how she lost her focus on what mattered most. When Jesus was a guest in Martha and Mary's home, Martha ran around frantically while her sister, Mary, sat at the Teacher's feet. Jesus gently reminded Martha, "You are worried and troubled about many things. But one thing is needed, and Mary has chosen that good part, which will not be taken away from her" (Luke 10:41–42). When I pause from the wild pace of my day (which I bring on myself most of the time), I hear Jesus whispering the same to me.

> WHEN I PAUSE FROM THE WILD PACE OF MY DAY, I HEAR JESUS WHISPERING THE SAME TO ME.

Dear heart, being still in the presence of the Lord is the *one thing* that matters. This is our reminder to choose the one thing, the best thing: Jesus. *He's* our treasure, so let's treasure Him.

I'm happy to report that that day without my phone was actually so freeing. No worries and no interruptions (until I saw the thirty texts at the end of the day!). And this truth about choosing the one best thing has also helped me in daily parenting; when one of my children is flustered,

"FEAR NOT,
FOR I HAVE
REDEEMED YOU;
I HAVE
CALLED YOU BY
YOUR NAME;
YOU ARE MINE."

ISAIAH 43:1

I'll say something like, "Sweetheart, you are worried and distracted with many things. Breathe. Rest in His love for you. It's going to be okay."

INVITING THE LORD'S PRESENCE INTO THIS MOMENT

Do you tend to lean more toward a Martha style or more toward the style of Mary? For me, it definitely depends on the day, the time of the month, or how emotionally spent I am—in other words, on how much margin I have to spare. What is unchanging, though, is Jesus' invitation to get away with Him. He modeled this in His own life, when He would regularly get away to be alone with His Father. In these few moments you have right now, settle in. Consider how Jesus spoke so tenderly with Martha, even repeating her name as evidence of His love for her. Maybe extend your hands in front of you in a posture of releasing control, relinquishing heartache, and receiving His shepherding and comfort.

SAY MY NAME

But now, thus says the Lord, who created you, O Jacob,
And He who formed you, O Israel:
"Fear not, for I have redeemed you;
I have called you by your name;
You are Mine."

ISAIAH 43:1

Lord, You know my name. Help me rest in Your love and affection for me. More than that, would You help me dwell with You and to know Your name? Your name is the highest name on earth, and it brings comfort just by speaking it. Change me from the inside out through the mention of Your name in my heart and on my lips. I love You, my Lord and my God. Amen.

WHEN WE WERE FIRST ENGAGED and then married, Levi and I got to lead a youth group in Albuquerque, New Mexico, leading around three hundred students. One night, I met one of the girls and asked her name, but I immediately forgot it. The next time I saw her, I didn't realize I had already met her and asked her name *again*. After the third time I still hadn't remembered her name. I just smiled and said, "Hey, girl!" instead.

I immediately felt so much shame and frustration with myself. It was like the little librarian in my brain (I imagine her as an old Filipino lady with a tight, high bun, thick-framed readers, a knee-length khaki pencil skirt, and a cream-colored sweater) who keeps track of all the information in there was off duty. She gave me nothing. I had no name to say.

In the aftermath of my disappointment with my own memory failure, I asked God to help me remember our students' names. To find out something about them that could help me remember. To connect the youth with other teenagers along with their leaders. *Goodness gracious*, it takes hard work to remember!

I have gotten much more intentional about learning and remembering people's names, but I still forget. (I hope my hugs will somehow wash away my sins of forgetfulness.) I have had a note in my phone for a few years now that is creatively labeled "NAMES OF PEOPLE." It has individual notes identifying people's names with places, along with something specific about them that will jog my memory about who they are. Or sometimes I will add a note in their contact information in my phone that gives me context about when and how I met them and what we talked about. That's on a good day, when I remember to do *that*!

Names matter to us. But they matter even more to God. God knows each of our names. He knows *your* name. And throughout Scripture, we hear Him addressing His people by name: Jacob, Martha, Samuel, Mary.

NAMES MATTER TO US. BUT THEY MATTER EVEN MORE TO GOD.

Sometimes God even said a person's name twice in a row: Moses, *Moses*. Abraham, *Abraham*. Saul, *Saul*. When it's said two times like that, you can almost hear the kindness and endearment in God's voice.

God speaks to us personally, and God spoke to Israel collectively. When Israel was suffering, God spoke tenderly to them, assuring them, "I have called you by your name; You are Mine" (Isaiah 43:1).

Sweet friend, God knows your name, and He is calling you by name. Can you hear that tender voice? God not only knows your name, but He sees you and loves you. Listen for His voice today.

INVITING THE LORD'S PRESENCE INTO THIS MOMENT

Father, I am turning my attention toward You right now. I look to You in faith, knowing that You see me fully—the good, the bad, the ugly, the beautiful. You see everything that it means to be me, and You love me. You adore me. You know my name, but You also know me so much deeper than that. I receive Your remarkable tenderness—tenderness that I can't receive from anyone else ever. I rest in Your unfailing love for me. I ask that it would truly change me from the inside out. Amen.

Fresh Mercy #2

FOLLOWING GOD EVERY SINGLE DAY

STRONG HANDS, STIRRED HEART

She girds herself with strength,
And strengthens her arms.
She perceives that her merchandise is good,
And her lamp does not go out by night.
She stretches out her hands to the distaff,
And her hand holds the spindle.
She extends her hand to the poor,
Yes, she reaches out her hands to the needy.

PROVERBS 31:17–20

God, I long to serve You and be used by You. Strengthen my spirit and my heart to serve others and to serve You and Your house. I surrender my heart to You. I offer my hands to be used for Your glory. Amen.

Have you seen my hands? In my opinion, I have *man hands*. I'm not complaining about the hands God gave me; I'm just saying I wouldn't describe them as petite, or slender, or feminine. I can't even wear rings comfortably because my fingers get puffy and expand really easily. So my "wedding ring" is Levi's name, in his handwriting, tattooed on my ring finger. All of the fun rings I've collected over the years sit sad and neglected in my drawer. (At least they have one another!) If you have lovely hands with slender fingers that look splendid with rings, I celebrate you! I also envy you. There, I said it.

The fact is, whether you're a professional hand model or you've got sturdy hands like mine, God's Word reminds us that our hands were made for a *purpose*. For strength. For offering kindness to those who need it. For generosity and showing God's love. And throughout the Scriptures, we're given glimpses of women who used their hands for good.

Ruth worked hard with her hands to provide for herself and her mother-in-law. We also read about the woman—or type of woman—described in Proverbs 31: "She stretches out her hands to the distaff, and her hand holds the spindle" (v. 19), speaking of how she made wool clothing. And we see beautiful, hardworking women in the book of Exodus: "All the women who were gifted artisans spun yarn with their hands, and brought what they had spun, of blue, purple, and scarlet, and fine linen" (Exodus 35:25).

These examples inspire me to be a woman with a heart that is stirred and willing to serve God. To give of whatever God has given me, to be a part of building the kingdom and His church, and to reach out to those in need.

The Proverbs 31 girl worked hard with her hands to make warm clothing for her family, but the offering of her hands was motivated by something else: a willing spirit and a stirred heart. She and these other women in the Bible (and plenty more) give us examples of what it looks like to work hard with a willing heart—willing and ready for what God had right in front of them. Taking care of their families, pouring into the house of God, and loving and serving people in need.

God didn't just give you strong hands (no matter what kind of hands you have); He has also put a heart inside you that wants to love and nurture and care for the people around you. And I believe that whether or not that comes naturally to you, *it is in you*—and God wants to use your heart and hands to glorify Him in ways that will leave you speechless.

INVITING THE LORD'S PRESENCE INTO THIS MOMENT

God has given each of us work to do—a unique and specific calling—and we honor Him when we offer our lives with a willing heart. Sometimes the work—cooking or caregiving or creating—is *literally* the work of our hands. Other times, the work may be prayer, or sharing wisdom, or giving in other ways with a generous spirit. Talk to God about the particular work He has assigned to your life. Consider areas of your life where you may not have realized that He's given you the opportunities and creativity to serve Him in a way that is unique to you. Thank Him. Tell Him you want to be even more aware of how He's moving around you and how He wants to include you in it.

"SHEESH MAGEESH" (EXCUSE MY LANGUAGE)

"A good man out of the good treasure of his heart brings forth good; and an evil man out of the evil treasure of his heart brings forth evil. For out of the abundance of the heart his mouth speaks."

LUKE 6:45

Lord, You know my heart even more than I do. And when I hear the words that leave my lips, I find out what's in there, too, for better or for worse. I confess that parts of my heart are ugly—not pleasing to You and not helpful to others. Forgive me, Father. I submit myself to You. Transform me from the inside out. Help me see what You see. Amen.

I DON'T KNOW WHEN IT STARTED, but there was a season in my life when the exclamation I'd use when I was frustrated was "Sheesh mageesh!" I'd say it to Levi, or I'd mutter it under my breath around the kids. It was meant to be cute and endearing, but it ended up becoming my own kind of curse word.

I can almost hear you say, "Jennie, are you serious? *This?* Come on, worse things have been said in frustration." And I hear it. You're right. But it became something that, for me, was just—not okay. What was yucky about it was my *tone*. Because what my tone revealed to me—and likely to the people in my life who heard it—was a heart that was troubled, selfish, unkind, and probably also pretty rude.

Recently, I made the decision to ditch this strange phrase, as well as the tone and attitude that came with it. It was the right choice for me, because I'd begun to realize that we communicate a lot through our tone. We communicate our frustration. Our contempt. Even our resentment. I think the light bulb came on for me when I began to hear my kids using my signature phrase. And once I began to notice it, I recognized what was in my heart when I spoke it. (Thank You, God, for children who repeat everything we say!)

When Jesus was speaking to a large crowd—which included His closest disciples—He encouraged them to realize what was in their own hearts. He said, "A good man out of the good treasure of his heart brings forth good; and an evil man out of the evil treasure of his heart brings forth evil. For out of the abundance of the heart his mouth speaks" (Luke 6:45). Maybe you've been in a tense conversation in which someone has said, "You don't know what's in my heart!" But Jesus is teaching that we actually *do* know, because our words reveal it. Ouch. Did you feel that sting too? Same.

I began trying to use an alternative to "Sheesh mageesh," namely to gently share how I'm feeling instead: "Levi, when you said that, I felt mad, because it seemed like you didn't care about how this affects me." And he would answer, "I'm sorry, sweetheart. I didn't mean to hurt you." Then we could make out, make up, and move forward.

What are the words that come out of your mouth? What do they tell you about something deeper that might be happening in your heart? Consider these things and bring them to Jesus; He will shepherd you and lead you in the right way.

HE WILL SHEPHERD YOU.

INVITING THE LORD'S PRESENCE INTO THIS MOMENT

"Search me, O God, and know my heart; try me, and know my anxieties; and see if there is any wicked way in me, and lead me in the way everlasting" (Psalm 139:23–24). Speak this prayer aloud to the Lord. Invite Him to examine what you may not be able to see about your own heart. Open your hands and ask Him to open your heart. Let Him be the heart surgeon that only He can be. Let Him begin the deep work. Practical applications here might include seeing a counselor, being vulnerable with your small group, or even opening up about an issue to your spouse or trusted mentor. We all have next steps in our walks with Jesus. Ask Him to show you what your personal next steps are with Him. And remember: He smiles when He thinks of you.

LOOK WITH LOVE

"For the Lord does not see as man sees; for man looks at the outward appearance, but the Lord looks at the heart."

1 SAMUEL 16:7

Lord God, help me surrender my will to Yours today. Help me to see things the way You see them. Give me the strength and grace and courage to put on Your lenses so that they would change how I see it all—so that Your lenses of love would help me see the hearts of others. Amen.

AFTER SHOWING OUR TICKETS, WE entered the concert and each received a light-up bracelet and paper 3D glasses. We attached the bracelets to our wrists and saved the glasses for whenever we would be instructed to put them on. When the music began, our bracelets lit up to correspond with certain musical cues of each song. It was spectacular. A whole stadium of strangers was united by these bracelets, which harmonized into a light symphony of joy and beauty.

But let's talk about the 3D glasses. I put mine on before we were instructed to. And as I placed them on my face, I audibly "wowed." Every single light beam that shone throughout the arena morphed into *hearts*, and it was so beautiful. I looked around, but no one else could see what I saw because they weren't yet looking through the same lenses I was. Liv and Daisy were sitting next to me, and when I suggested they put on the glasses, we were finally seeing the same thing.

The experience reminded me that we look at our own lives and the lives of others through filtered lenses. It also reminded me that God's vision—of us, of our lives—is much different from the way *we* see things. He sees our hearts. And then God filters what He sees through His love and kindness and tenderness and truth. First Samuel 16:7 reminds us, "For the LORD does not see as man sees; for man looks at the outward appearance, but the LORD looks at the heart" (v. 7).

Left to ourselves, we can love and be kind—for a time. But then we get tired and let down our guards and become easily irritated with the humanness of others. Or someone hurts us. Or it's that time of the month when hormone levels are fluctuating and everyone irritates us and we just have nothing more to give. Our love runs out. These are the moments when we need to surrender to our Savior, whose love is perfect and pure and will never run out. God welcomes us today to ask for His view, His perspective, His vision. He invites us to see our lives, and the lives of the people around us, with *His eyes*. When we put on His lenses—His love glasses—we can finally see others and ourselves through the filter of truth.

INVITING THE LORD'S PRESENCE INTO THIS MOMENT

God, You know me inside and out. And You know how I see others. I see their broken places. I can focus on their faults. I fail to see the ways in which they are beloved by You. God, help me to see the way You see: with love, with kindness, with tenderness, with forgiveness, with truth. Let me focus on the deep work You are doing in my heart. It's not a pretty process or even desirable, but it's deep. It's Your handiwork. The most important thing to remember is that You are faithful. You began the work in me, and You will continue to work, and then finish it. Amen.

P.S.

God used this same verse to speak deeply into my heart when I was thirteen years old: "For the Lord does not see as man sees; for man looks

He who follows righteousness and mercy finds life, righteousness, and honor.

Proverbs 21:21

at the outward appearance, but the LORD looks at the heart" (1 Samuel 16:7).

I was really struggling with my physical appearance. I had terrible acne that covered my face, and I felt so ugly—and so *not* beautiful. I remember being on vacation with my family once when I encountered this verse in my evening Bible reading, and though it felt like the whole room was dark, it was as if God had shone a beam of light right on this line.

What?! I remember thinking. What people may focus on is not how God sees us. In that moment, I realized that He sees deeper than skin, and quite frankly, that's what really matters. I cried. I felt myself melting into His love. And I felt so free to also focus on my heart and let Him build me up and strengthen me from the inside out.

My acne was still there, and I still didn't feel outwardly pretty, but my perspective changed then. My heart was beautiful, and I knew God could work in me to make me even more beautiful.

Inner beauty is a beauty that grows.

I wish I could say that was a one-and-done solution and that I never struggled with body image or feeling ugly ever again, but that's just not true or realistic for us humans. It is still a struggle, especially on those days when my pants fit differently—and not a "good" kind of different. Or when I compare myself to another woman and how fit she is. Or when I just look at the outside of me. It can be disheartening. But I often go back to that moment in my first teenage year, when God showed up to a young and naïve version of me and spoke His love and His perspective over my life. And I speak it over you today—whether you're thirteen, thirty-one, fifty-six, or eighty-three: Whatever your age, your beauty comes from within.

SPEAKING TO A KING

Let no corrupt word proceed out of your mouth, but what is good for necessary edification, that it may impart grace to the hearers.

EPHESIANS 4:29

Dear God, I pray over the men in my life—my husband, son, brothers, co-workers, and friends. Lord, strengthen them. Bless them. Give me the courage and love and tenderness to speak to them and about them in a way that blesses You and honors both You and them. Amen.

THERE ARE PLENTY OF JOBS in which you get to—or have to—hear other people's conversations. Those who work the doors at hotels overhear all kinds of things. Those who clean homes, or work in coffee shops, or wait tables. The barber or hairstylist or makeup artist. When I was a server at Macaroni Grill, I sometimes heard more than I wanted to.

One evening I was waiting on four women—two older and two younger. Every time I passed by their table or refilled their drinks, I heard them "men bashing," saying really unkind things about their husbands. The younger ones would whine, "It's all his fault," or "He's such a jerk." On one pass-by, I heard one of the older women instructing, "Sometimes you just have to tell them what to do."

Now you might be thinking, *Gosh, Jennie, you're so nosy*. Ha-ha! Heard! I also admit that I didn't know the context of the conversations. Maybe those husbands *were* awful and horrible and mean. I'll never know.

But what I *do* know is that the conversation at that table opened my eyes. It made me think about the conversations that *I* have with other women, whether they're married or single. If a woman shares something intimate and difficult with me, I want to be a good listener. But I also want to speak life and truth over the people who trust me enough to share hard things. I want to speak life both *to* my husband and *about* my husband, even when he's not around. I actually gleaned that idea from Levi when he once preached about the ways in which we speak to the men in our lives—a spouse, a brother, a colleague, a friend. Whether we speak to the king inside that man or to the fool, the one we speak to will rise up. (Life-changing!)

WHETHER WE SPEAK TO THE KING INSIDE THAT MAN OR TO THE FOOL, THE ONE WE SPEAK TO WILL RISE UP.

Who are the men in your life? Husband, brother, son, father? He may be someone you supervise at work or someone who might lead a team at your church. I encourage you to recognize the king inside each one. Speak life. Speak to who God has called them to rise up to be, not to how they might be living now. Speak to the king, not to the fool.

INVITING THE LORD'S PRESENCE INTO THIS MOMENT

Take a moment to pray over the men in your life: a father, grandfather, brother, husband, son, friend, boyfriend, fiancé, in-law. If it's a strained relationship, ask God to help you see them the way He does. Maybe he is someone who has hurt you. I'm not saying you need to reach out to this person, but just start with prayer. God will shepherd you into what's next. Ask Him to help you see and speak to the king inside of that man, not the fool. Ask God to strengthen and bless him. Ask Him to grow you into the kind of woman who speaks life and blessing and hope and peace over the guys in her life.

SPEAK KINDLY TO . . . YOU

She also rises while it is yet night,
And provides food for her household,
And a portion for her maidservants. . . .
She opens her mouth with wisdom,
And on her tongue is the law of kindness.

PROVERBS 31:15, 26

Father, I confess that I'm weak and needy and frail, but You, O Lord, are strong. I'm sorry for how I tend to make my life all about me. I'm sorry for my attitude and for the complaining I do—both in my heart and out loud. Forgive me, Lord. Thank You for such amazing grace. Thank You for such unconditional love. Amen.

MOST DAYS AROUND 4:30 P.M. or so, one of my children or my husband will ask the most dreaded question I can hear: "What's for dinner?" At the sound of this innocent query, I start sweating. I want to not only have the answer ready but also give them the answer they're looking for: "Oh yes, I *definitely* know what's for dinner, and I *definitely* know you will love it!" How is it always a surprise to me that it's dinnertime *again*, and I have failed to plan?

To be fair, the question is legit. I do love to cook and have found that I actually *can* cook (although baking is a whole different story—my daughter Clover outbakes me, and I'm so okay with that), but the planning and prepping part is what gets me. Every. Single. Time. I go through spurts of being on it, and then not. So instead of answering the question, I pause, say a few *uhs* and *hmms* and *wells*, and I begin to say something but then trail off when I see they have lost interest. Then the mad dash to really figure it out begins. Thoughts like these immediately build up in my mind: *Why didn't you plan something? Be better, Jennie! I'm just a terrible planner and a bad cook, so let's just eat out!*

I really do need to plan better, and I really do need a system, but until the day comes when I get ahold of myself and my life and my meal planning, I can encourage myself rather than berate myself. I can say something kinder like, *It's okay, Jennie. You made a great meal last night, so leftovers are totally an option.* Or, *You're growing and getting better. You can do this. Let's see what you can come up with in the next hour!*

When we read about the woman in Proverbs 31, it can be tempting to be hard on ourselves. But this woman is more than a savvy entrepreneur and a culinary genius. Proverbs 31:26 announces, "She opens her mouth with wisdom, and on her tongue is the law of kindness." I want you to hear that the kindness on her tongue is not just for others; it's for her too. And it's for *you*. And me.

Your life and mine may differ, but whatever your last-minute equivalent of "Taco Bell drive-through" is, I want to remind you to speak kindly to yourself. If you struggle in some of the ways I do, be gentle with yourself. Keep trying. And give yourself the space to grow. God will use that space to create some beautiful flourishing.

GIVE YOURSELF THE SPACE TO GROW.

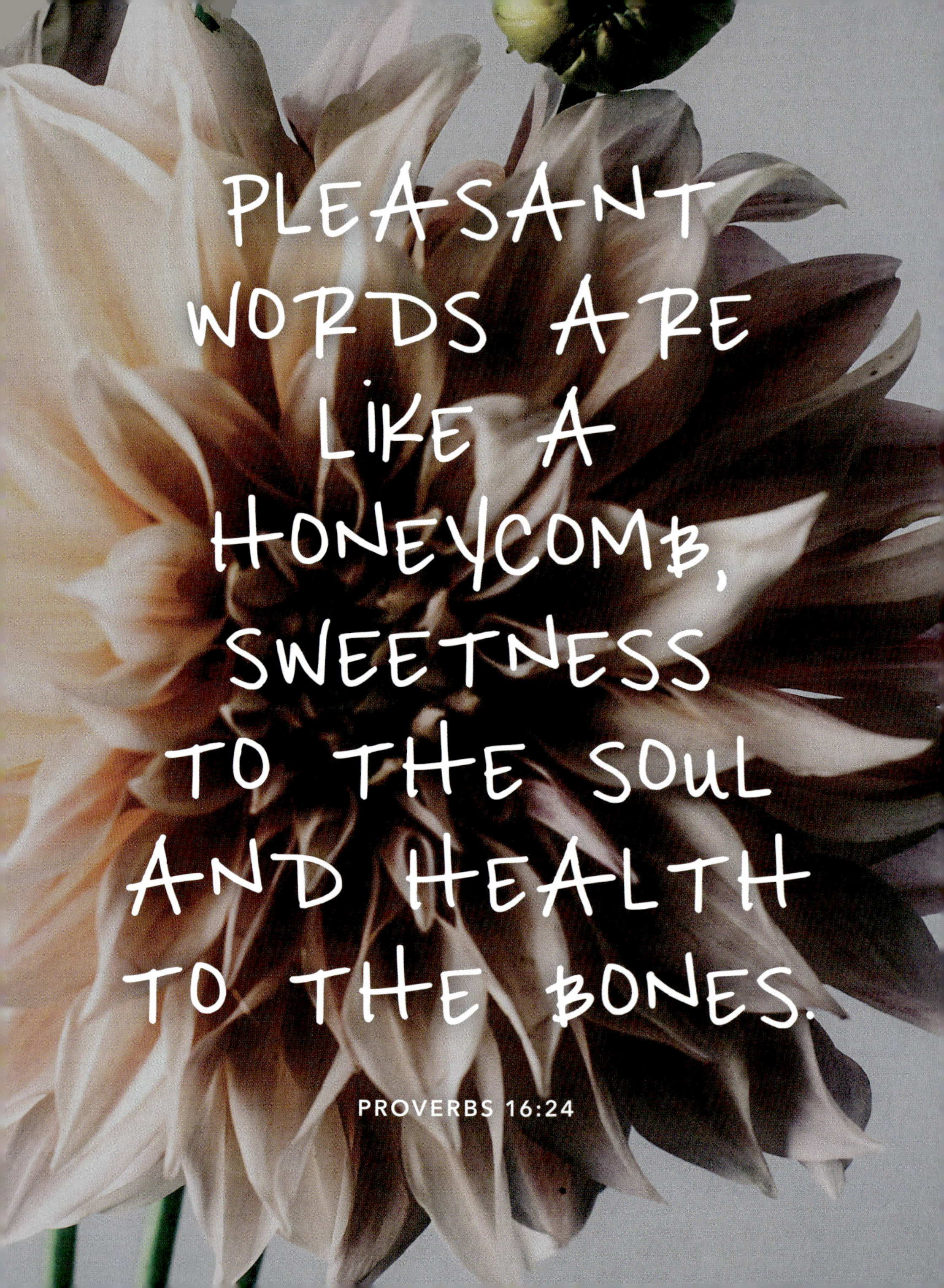

PLEASANT WORDS ARE LIKE A HONEYCOMB, SWEETNESS TO THE SOUL AND HEALTH TO THE BONES.

PROVERBS 16:24

INVITING THE LORD'S PRESENCE INTO THIS MOMENT

We all are fighting through some of our weaknesses and mess-ups and mistakes. Just like I know the areas where I'm still learning to find my footing, you know the areas where you struggle too—perhaps even daily. Take a moment to write about some of these areas. Name those pinch points and bring them before the Lord. You might think it's a tiny or insignificant thing, but it all matters to the God who created you and cares for you. Sit in His goodness and grace and ask Him to help you speak to yourself the way you would encourage a dear friend.

PRAY LIKE THIS

"In this manner, therefore, pray:
Our Father in heaven,
Hallowed be Your name.
Your kingdom come.
Your will be done
On earth as it is in heaven.
Give us this day our daily bread.
And forgive us our debts,
As we forgive our debtors.
And do not lead us into temptation,
But deliver us from the evil one."

MATTHEW 6:9–13

Good morning, Lord! Thank You for a brand-new day. I ask You for a fresh filling of fuel, of the Holy Spirit, of power, of passion to live for You. Father, I long to meet with You—in the quiet and on the run—and hear Your voice. Teach me how to pray. Speak, Lord, for Your servant is listening. Amen.

I love that Jesus taught His disciples how to pray. He had just taught them not to pray like the spiritual leaders who were out there on the street corners causing a scene, trying to *be* seen. He coached them instead to pray privately, in their closets. And then He went one step further and *modeled* prayer for them, saying, "In this manner, therefore, pray" (Matthew 6:9). Basically, Jesus told them how to pray and then said, "Check it out—watch and learn."

When I was a teenager, my youth pastor did something similar. He taught us an easy way to pray, using the mnemonic of *ACTS*. *A* was for *Adoration*, *C* was for *Confession*, *T* was for *Thanksgiving*, and *S* was for *Supplication*. All those years ago, this made an imprint on my heart. And I am so grateful for a simple way to approach prayer. This isn't the only way, by any means, but it's a really good reminder that prayer is more simple than we can make it out to be.

SOMETIMES JUST STARTING IS THE HARDEST PART.

Sometimes just starting is the hardest part. You might wonder, *Do I thank Him first, or do I ask Him for something first? Do I just sit still and know that He is God?* I love how the Lord's Prayer begins: "Our Father in heaven, hallowed be Your name." It all begins with

Him. Who He is. Where He is, and how holy He is. *Boom.* Always a great place to start.

The prayer begins as we offer our praise, or *adoration*, to God. This could be with words, a song, or silence. Then we humble ourselves with *confession*, acknowledging where we've sinned and confessing our desperate need for Him in the day and in the moment. Then we give *thanks*, for anything and everything—including forgiveness for what we just confessed. And finally: *supplication*. Like children going to a parent they trust, we ask God for what we need. This word in the Greek is *deésis*, which is found in Philippians 4:6 and speaks to a pleading, an imploring, an intense kind of asking. Kind of like running to God expectantly and praying with our guts, our abs, with *everything*.

What it really comes down to isn't the words you speak or the phrasing or the formula—it's the relationship you have with your heavenly Father. The point is that He wants to meet with you, and the longing of your heart should be an increasing desire to be in His presence. Because that's where your strength comes from: time with your Savior.

Sweet friend, if you find yourself in a rut in your prayer life, this simple way of praying might help jump-start your conversations with God. It has definitely helped me in my life and continues to do so, even today.

INVITING THE LORD'S PRESENCE INTO THIS MOMENT

I really hope these two templates for prayer—the Lord's Prayer, which Jesus used, and the ACTS flow—are helpful as you spend time with God today. Maybe set a timer on your phone, put it out of reach, and linger in His presence as He leads you in prayer.

WORDS OF THE WISE

"Either make the tree good and its fruit good, or else make the tree bad and its fruit bad; for a tree is known by its fruit. . . . A good man out of the good treasure of his heart brings forth good things, and an evil man out of the evil treasure brings forth evil things."

MATTHEW 12:33, 35

O Lord, would You build up the good treasure in my heart today? As I wait on You, letting Your Word lead me and set the pace for my life, would You create in me a clean heart, O God, and renew a right spirit within me? Amen.

FEET ARE SO STRANGE TO me. I don't like looking at them, but then, on the other hand, I am also mesmerized by them and can't not stare. Everyone's feet are so different. Some people have really beautiful feet, but I feel like most people don't. I know God made us all beautiful, and He made our feet, but wow, thank God for shoes. Okay, this is a dramatic and weird opinion, and I probably shouldn't even be bringing this up.

But early in our marriage, Levi and I were sitting on the couch together, snuggling and watching a movie, when I blurted out, "Levi, I love you, but I only tolerate your feet." (I actually can't believe I'm admitting this for the world to see!) I immediately regretted my words and wished I hadn't said them, aware that I should have thought a little first about how that would make him feel. Or at the very least, about how it would have made *me* feel to hear those words. *Come on, Jennie, you don't have to say* everything *you think out loud!*

If I could take that one back, I would!

In Proverbs 31:26, the godly woman is described this way: "She opens her mouth with wisdom, and on her tongue is the law of kindness." That girl? That's who I want to be. Jesus' words remind me that the way to become the woman who speaks with wisdom and kindness is to be a woman who *stores* wisdom and kindness in her heart.

What it comes down to is remembering that whatever comes out of our mouths begins in our hearts. And there's either good treasure stored in there or there's evil. I know that one way to store good treasure is to fill up on God's Word. I want to grow in my meditation on it and want to learn more of it, but I also want to let it change me more. I want it to help me see how my words affect others—for better or for worse.

When I let the Holy Spirit lead, I can take a second, ask Him for wisdom and help and love, and then walk in the way He leads me. And then I hopefully won't stick my foot in my mouth as much either! (Also, *gross*!)

INVITING THE LORD'S PRESENCE INTO THIS MOMENT

James talked about the tongue and how much trouble it can be. "With it we bless our God and Father, and with it we curse men, who have been made in the similitude of God" (James 3:9). "How can this be?" he essentially asked. We can sometimes watch words come out of our mouths in slow motion, usually while we wish we could retrieve them before they hit someone's ears and then their heart.

Paul also taught that one of the fruits of the Spirit is self-control (Galatians 5:23). This might be a great little moment to bring the issue of our tongue before the Lord. Re-surrender your heart to Him. Admit your need for Him. Acknowledge your inner struggle to practice self-control with your words. Ask Him to help you grow in this area, giving *Him* control over your self-control. He wants to be your strength in this. He wants the "words of [your] mouth and this meditation of [your] heart [to] be acceptable in [His] sight" (Psalm 19:14).

SWEET HONEYCOMB

The wise in heart will be called prudent,
And sweetness of the lips increases learning.
Understanding is a wellspring of life to him who has it.
But the correction of fools is folly.
The heart of the wise teaches his mouth,
And adds learning to his lips.
Pleasant words are like a honeycomb,
Sweetness to the soul and health to the bones.

PROVERBS 16:21–24

Lord, You know that I long to speak with kindness, yet I confess that I'm weak. But You are strong. In the midst of the rush of my daily life today, teach me to offer words spoken with gentleness and love. Help me, Lord. Amen.

FAMILY

WHEN OUR DAUGHTERS ALIVIA AND Lenya were four and two years old and Levi and I took an opportunity to travel to California—just the two of us. And before this, I hadn't been away from our girls . . . *ever.*

Levi had been pastoring Fresh Life in Kalispell, Montana, for about three years when we had the chance to spend some time together. The place where we stayed had an ocean view that was stunning. We were able to get away because family and friends back in Montana were taking care of the girls. For the first time since having children, there were no extra little humans running around constantly needing us. We were free to focus on each other. And it was just so luxurious, all of it!

During a few of those leisurely hours away, in my times with the Lord, I started to notice a *theme* in what He was showing me. One morning, God seemed to be highlighting the verse Proverbs 16:21 to me: "The wise in heart will be called prudent, and sweetness of the lips increases learning." Later in the day, the Spirit led me to a passage a few verses down: "Pleasant words are like a honeycomb, sweetness to the soul and health to the bones" (Proverbs 16:24).

Okay, God, I hear You. I'm listening!

It almost felt like God had been waiting to get my attention, and now He finally had it. Our lives were so full with ministry and the girls—especially Lenya's health challenges and her new feeding tube—that it had been hard to get still with God without falling asleep or being pulled in another direction. And yet, there on the beach, it felt like God was reminding me—in that place of beauty and with the rhythm of the waves—to practice kindness when I returned to my regularly scheduled life, to use pleasant words to bring sweetness to my soul and the souls of others. To bring health to my bones *and* to the bones of those around me.

God was so kind to speak to me through His Word, opening my eyes to what it looks like to be transformed to be more like Jesus. My prayer that day was simple: *I am weak, but You are strong. On my own, I can tend to be sour and bitter, but help me cling to Your truth, which brings sweetness. I need You, Lord.*

INVITING THE LORD'S PRESENCE INTO THIS MOMENT

I don't think it comes naturally to us to pause and listen to the words that leave our lips. But sometimes God intervenes with grace and gives us a *heart check*. If we're aware of it and we lean in, deep heart work can happen.

Consider assessing the past few days and thinking about the words you have spoken. Ask God to help you see how He might be wanting to instill an even deeper dependence on His Word in you, thus creating a deeper sweetness that over time will spill out from your mouth.

> *Let it be, Lord, from Your heart to ours, and to others through our words. Amen.*

Fresh Mercy #3

TRUSTING GOD IN EVERYTHING

GOD CARES FOR YOU

For You formed my inward parts;
You covered me in my mother's womb.
I will praise You, for I am fearfully and wonderfully made;
Marvelous are Your works,
And that my soul knows very well. . . .
Your eyes saw my substance, being yet unformed.
And in Your book they all were written,
The days fashioned for me,
When as yet there were none of them.

PSALM 139:13–14, 16

O Lord, calm my anxious heart. Lord, Your will be done! You give and You take away—I bless Your name! God, You promise that I can cast my burdens on You, and I trust that You will sustain me. I will listen, I will trust, and I will obey. I trust in Your timing and in Your providence. Amen.

MY MENSTRUAL MATH TOLD ME that Levi and I had conceived our daughter during makeup sex after a big fight on a cold winter night. TMI? Probably. Yet on the morning when Levi and I were heading to the doctor to confirm our pregnancy, I felt really anxious. I'd taken a pregnancy test five days earlier and gotten the good news that we were expecting. And yet part of me was worried that the test had been wrong, and that I wasn't really pregnant. Another part feared that in those few days, I'd miscarried without even knowing it.

THIS LITTLE EXPERIENCE REMINDED ME THAT I REALLY COULD TRUST GOD WITH EVERYTHING. EVERY. LITTLE. THING.

That morning, in the middle of all my feelings, I'd read Psalm 139. And that day it had sort of a double meaning: "For You formed my inward parts; You covered me in my mother's womb" (v. 13). Not only did God hold the potential life that had been growing inside me in His tender care, but God also held my own life in His hands. This helped me to release the situation to God in the moment.

Of course, we were relieved when the doctor confirmed the good news that we were expecting. This baby would be due to arrive in the second week of October. God was knitting her together and designing her in my womb, and there was nothing I could do to control it. He was the One who had seen fit to show us that it was time for us to have a baby. This little experience reminded me that I really could trust God with *everything.* Every. Little. Thing. And that includes every tiny human growing in the womb. If the doctor had told us otherwise, that would've also been the Lord's timing. He knows it all, and He is concerned with me and all the burdens—small or large—that I carry.

Psalm 139 reminds us that He is intimately concerned with the details of our lives. Dear one, do you believe that God cares about the things you care about, and that He welcomes you to lay your burdens on Him, "casting all your care upon Him, for He cares for you" (1 Peter 5:7)?

INVITING THE LORD'S PRESENCE INTO THIS MOMENT

Think about what you need today. Take a moment and write these needs down or make a note in your phone. Have you been carrying these things around, trying to handle them on your own or manage them without even knowing it? Ask God for the awareness to see what you need, and to release it to Him. He sees. He knows. And He is able—*more* than able. Sit for a moment and talk with God about what you need. Renew your trust in Him, and tell Him so. He longs to be the One you run to with all the things.

OVERWHELMED

Therefore humble yourselves under the mighty hand of God, that He may exalt you in due time, casting all your care upon Him, for He cares for you.

1 PETER 5:6–7

God, You know I need You so much. You know my heart, my mind, my worries, my anxieties, and my frustrations. You search me and know me. I cry out to You! I need You, but I haven't clung to You like I should. Help me to know Your loving-kindness in the morning. Thank You for sustaining me. Amen.

SOMETIMES THINGS GET REALLY BAD. You know what I mean. Like *really* bad—and it usually comes out of nowhere.

Our nine-month-old daughter, Lenya, wasn't eating well and was losing a lot of weight. Developmentally, her progress was slowing. Her health seemed to be spiraling downward fast, and we had no idea what was wrong. Because we didn't have the resources we needed in our small town at the time, her doctor told us to get to Spokane, Washington, as soon as possible. Levi and I drove four hours to take her for an evaluation with a gastroenterologist at a feeding and growth clinic. Within hours, they admitted our little one to Spokane's children's hospital. We had planned to stay just one night, but we ended up staying there for five.

When Lenya was diagnosed with "failure to thrive," I felt like a failure as a mom. But we discovered in the hospital that she had several severe allergies. What we could see on the outside of her body—rashes, physical weakness—was originating inside her body, affecting her eating and therefore her growth. We learned she was allergic to wheat, soy, cow's milk, eggs, chicken, peanuts, cashews, hazelnuts, and almonds. About a month later, the doctors inserted a port into her stomach so we could feed her with a feeding tube, and she was finally able to get the nourishment she needed. Still, it was all overwhelming and exhausting.

One evening, a few months after we were back home, I broke down and wept. The year Lenya was diagnosed was also the year when Levi broke his femur, and between constant caregiving and the growing medical bills, I felt like I was drowning. But I also knew that God had His eyes on me and that He was with me. Peter exhorted the early church to cast "all your care upon Him, for He cares for you" (1 Peter 5:7). In the midst of being completely overwhelmed, I turned to God, and He met me. He held me *and* the things I was carrying. And then I had to keep going to Him. And keep surrendering to Him. It was a pretty constant thing, and it dawned on me that this was the point: running to Him with my cares, because He cares for me. That's the point of it all!

I don't know what you're carrying today, but I know it's not too much for God. Whether it's health matters, finances, relationships, or something else that is weighing you down, I encourage you to take your burdens to the One who cares for you today. And then, to keep going to Him.

INVITING THE LORD'S PRESENCE INTO THIS MOMENT

What feels heavy for you in this season? It might literally be a physically heavy load. Or it might be a concern you're carrying that can feel just as weighty because it's heavy on your heart, soul, and mind. Spend some time offering God the burdens you are hauling around: people, situations, worries, diagnoses, needs. He created you and knows you. Rest in His arms, and submit to His shepherding. Let Him carry you as He cares for you. And then, keep letting Him carry you.

FAITH TO GIVE

So He called His disciples to Himself and said to them, "Assuredly, I say to you that this poor widow has put in more than all those who have given to the treasury; for they all put in out of their abundance, but she out of her poverty put in all that she had, her whole livelihood."

MARK 12:43–44

Lord, grow me in being faithful and wise. You know I haven't given a tithe in a month, and now I feel like I can't catch up. Lord, this is the first time I haven't tithed. I want to keep giving and keep surrendering and keep taking risks, even when it doesn't make sense. Amen.

THERE WAS A TIME IN my journey when it became really difficult to tithe, to give God a tenth of all my earnings. Levi was working at our church, and I was a server at Macaroni Grill, and the income was not brimming over. In that season, I poured my heart out to God in my journal: *Lord God, I look to You right now. My heart is overwhelmed with finances, with needing to buy birthday presents for family,* still *needing to send out Christmas cards, getting my license . . . but You lead me to the Rock that is higher than I.*

It was early in our marriage, and God had been so good to us, blessing us even though money was tight. I continued in my journal: *Father, I know You will provide for our needs this month, and I know that You are my Shepherd. So I shall not want.* As I wrote, I breathed a prayer that I could be as trusting as the psalmist was.

In that moment, I was reminded of today's scripture. These people in the church were giving their gifts to God at the altar as Jesus watched. There were very wealthy men who gave, but Jesus wasn't impressed. (Wow, that's sobering.) Why? Because these men didn't give with *faith.* There was also a woman there who had nothing but two tiny coins that didn't amount to anything of value. And yet she gave. She literally gave everything she had. What was it about this woman's speck of a gift that caused Jesus to nudge His disciples with a glimmer in His eye? Her faith. There was faith in this offering, and it made Jesus marvel.

In the midst of the financial limitations Levi and I faced in those early days of marriage, I knew I wanted to be like this woman. I wanted that heart full of faith. And so I committed in my heart to tithe and give generously with a faith that would wow Jesus. We had already committed to bringing a tithe to God with any increase He blessed us with, but this moment of growth was *in my own heart.*

THERE WAS FAITH IN THIS OFFERING, AND IT MADE JESUS MARVEL.

God was so kind and gentle to remind me to trust Him with everything, and through this, He helped strengthen my faith and taught me to trust Him in a fresh way—to give Him my first and my best and to let Him bless the rest as He saw fit! He is so good and so wise to work this in the minds of His kids.

INVITING THE LORD'S PRESENCE INTO THIS MOMENT

God, thank You for what You've entrusted to me. All that I have is Yours. Lord, I am trusting You to meet my needs this day, this month, this year. What's mine is Yours. As I consider the gifts You've given, inspire and equip me to be as generous as the poor widow who gave You everything she had with a heart of deep faith in her good God. Amen.

HOPE IN GOD

Why are you cast down, O my soul?
And why are you so disquieted within me?
Hope in God;
For I shall yet praise Him,
The help of my countenance and my God.

PSALM 42:11

Good morning, Lord! Help me to find my encouragement today in You. Remind me to hope in You and to trust in You. Help me see the version of me who has hope and who is in her right mind. Give me Your strength to not give up. Amen.

THE YEAR OF OUR TWENTIETH wedding anniversary, Levi and I celebrated by taking a trip together that we had dreamed of for a long time. With much planning and prepping (on Levi's part), we found ourselves in Florence, Italy.

One night we were enjoying dinner at a restaurant that had seating outdoors on the street. The day before, I'd had a PMDD (premenstrual dysphoric disorder) episode, where I melted down emotionally with Levi at a meal. I felt sad, insecure, hurting, confused. And I was mad at myself because here we were on a romantic getaway, and why couldn't I get control of myself?! *Jennie, really?!* But on this particular night at dinner, we were processing through what had happened the day before. I was sharing how I'd felt so much shame and confusion and heartache, the kind that

feels like it's choking you. I remember, through my tears, looking across the street at the logo of a little shop on its glass door. (It's funny the things you fixate on and remember when you're in an emotional moment.) We continued our conversation, walking back to the hotel hand in hand, Levi showing me such grace and kindness.

IT'S FUNNY THE THINGS YOU FIXATE ON AND REMEMBER WHEN YOU'RE IN AN EMOTIONAL MOMENT.

The next day, Levi asked if there was anything I wanted to do, and I mentioned how a manicure would be so lovely, and, in classic Levi fashion, with a look that said, *On it!* he proceeded to find the best manicure place near us and then booked a spot for me. About twenty minutes into my appointment, I looked up and saw a logo that was familiar to me. I was so confused as to how I knew this logo all the way in Italy, but as I kept looking and then peered through the window to the other side of the street, I noticed the plant that had been hanging down over my shoulder at the restaurant the previous evening, touching my hair all throughout our dinner.

Recalling the conversation with Levi, I pictured us at that same table the night before. I could see myself sitting there, and I thought about what I would've encouraged myself with if I'd been feeling like the woman I was that day in the nail salon: calm, strong, levelheaded, understanding.

In these moments, when I'm overwhelmed by my emotions and thoughts and insecurities, I recall the version of myself sitting across the street, getting her nails done. She gently assures me, *Jennie, it's going to be okay. Fight for the truth in your perspective right now. Why are you so discouraged? Hope in God.*

When David spoke this to himself in Psalm 42:11, he did something very similar, asking of himself, "Why are you cast down, O my soul? And why are you disquieted within me?" The stronger version of David reminded the discouraged version, "*Hope* in God." And that's what I knew God was giving me a glimpse of in this moment, helping me have a better view in future moments.

INVITING THE LORD'S PRESENCE INTO THIS MOMENT

Lord, thank You that it's no surprise to You that there are two versions of me. There are days when I wake up in the morning full of faith and hope, and Your fresh mercies flood over me in a happy way. And then there are other days when—in the midst of my best efforts—I feel so discouraged and undeserving of Your fresh mercies, and usually I have no idea why. God, as I unburden my soul to You and give you the discouragement that threatens to overwhelm me, I listen for Your voice, wait on You, and choose to hope in You alone. Amen.

DEPENDING ON JESUS

I know how to be abased, and I know how to abound. Everywhere and in all things I have learned both to be full and to be hungry, both to abound and to suffer need. I can do all things through Christ who strengthens me.

PHILIPPIANS 4:12–13

Lord God, it's been hard, but my eyes have been opened. As a result, I'm more dependent on Christ than ever, more in love with Levi than ever, and hopefully a little more like Jesus than before. Thank You, God! Amen.

After one of our first big outreach events at Fresh Life Church, Levi and a friend took a visiting pastor friend snowmobiling. Levi loves to give visiting guests the "Montana experience," whether it's an early summer hike, dogsledding, or horseback riding. It brings us so much joy to get to bless people who work hard to serve the Lord. We hope that as they minister here, they get a little rest and a taste of the beauty of Big Sky Country.

But on this day, during what was supposed to be a fun afternoon with friends, while trying to clear a hill, Levi's leg hit the handlebars and he broke his femur. (Insert desperation-face emoji here.) Two days after surgery, Levi was released from the hospital. Because our home at that time had two sets of mega-stairs—one set to get to our room and another set just to get to the main floor—we moved in with friends for that recovery period, which turned out to be for a month (thank you, Rays!). But this piece of the story isn't about him; it's about me.

I'll just say this: Levi was on intense pain meds that made him emotional, sometimes irrational, and moody. Basically, he became like me on a regular day. (I receive that burn I just gave myself.) Suddenly I was forced to be the grounded, gracious, rational one in the relationship. (Yes, it's hard to admit that!) And during that healing season, I began to learn even more of what God had been showing me for years: what it means to love unconditionally.

From my perspective, during that recovery period, I was working my tail off to help him with everything. From his perspective, it appeared that I hated it and was doing it only out of obligation. But what was so hard and painful and horrible for Levi ended up being something that really transformed me. It *was* hard to care for him on top of caring for the girls. But having that experience opened my eyes to the ways that my own moods had been impacting my family in big ways. And God used that experience—which neither of us would have chosen—to help me see the difficult side of myself and to realize what Levi was witnessing in me.

Although it was hard to admit how I had been living, one result of that mess was that I learned more of what it means to be dependent on Christ. That unwelcome opportunity to see myself more clearly—especially the parts of me that I wouldn't let most people see, besides Levi and my daughters and God—gave me the opportunity to lean on Him, moment by moment, for vision and strength. I've been growing in practicing His presence in all the moments, one by one, little by little, and, as a result, I think it deepened me specifically in that season.

THEREFORE HUMBLE YOURSELVES UNDER THE MIGHTY HAND OF GOD, THAT HE MAY EXALT YOU IN DUE TIME, CASTING ALL YOUR CARE UPON HIM, FOR HE CARES FOR YOU.

1 PETER 5:6–7

When Paul told the early believers that he could do all things through Christ who gave him strength, that wasn't a pep talk before some state athletic championship game. It was his declaration that he had seen it all—plenty, lack, disaster—and, in it all, he could overcome because of Christ's strength, whether the Philippian church gave generously and supported him on the road or not. He witnessed God's provision in every sense of the word, in every season of his life.

Sweet one, I fully believe that the circumstance you find yourself in today, especially if it's painful, might be a way in which God is holding a mirror up to you. Not in a condescending or shame-filled way, but in the loving way only He operates in—helping us to see the dark parts of us that He wants to shine His light into and opening our eyes to see the depth of beauty and flourishing He wants to continue to bring out of our lives. He will provide for you. He will teach you. And He will enable you to do all the things He is calling you to do, right now, today.

INVITING THE LORD'S PRESENCE INTO THIS MOMENT

Every day, God welcomes us to be transformed more and more into the image of Christ. And the truth is that it rarely happens when everything in our lives is going really well. Usually, it's in the challenges and struggles and heartache we face that our character is transformed. In this moment, offer God what is difficult in your life right now. Tell Him what hurts. Tell Him everything. He wants you to run to Him. He's the answer to your every need and ache and pain. Invite Him to use this difficulty to make you more like Jesus. And give Him the space to give you His rest.

GRACE AND GRIT

He who has begun a good work in you will complete it until the day of Jesus Christ.

PHILIPPIANS 1:6

God, You know me. Inside and out, You know me. You know how I am. You know that I start with big energy, but I often get distracted. I lose momentum. I procrastinate. Be my Helper. I am trusting that You will complete the good work You've started in me, and that today is part of that beautiful work. Amen.

I'M A REALLY GREAT STARTER. I start reading books. I start writing in journals. I start workout regimens. I start the kids' school year strong, planning and cooking healthy meals for my family. I could go on and on about how good of a starter I am.

What about finishing? you may ask. Do I complete what I start? Well, that's a different story. It's not that I *can't* finish; it's just that—among other things—I get distracted. So I lose the momentum. And when something gets hard, I start procrastinating. Something may get put on my to-do list, but then it ends up being on that list for a very long time. And slowly, eventually, I forget about it. The struggle is real. My struggle is real. And I'm guessing, while it's probably somewhat different, your struggle is too.

I'm thankful that the Lord gives us room to grow and opportunities to better steward what He has given us. I'm also thankful for a high-capacity husband who helps me with time management. I take my time, but he *takes* his time, and he knows exactly what he does with every minute. I'm also thankful for the people in my life who challenge me, whose very lives inspire me to grow and be strong. When it comes to reading books and cooking meals, I'm committed to working hard to get it done.

THE LORD GIVES US ROOM TO GROW.

But when it comes to salvation? I don't have to stress about *that*! And that's because I am confident that the One who started that work in me is going to complete it. My job is to believe and trust, knowing that God is working in me, even now. Because of what Jesus has done, I don't have to waste one moment being concerned about my salvation. And sanctification? That is, being made to look more and more like Jesus? I am not alone in that either.

Paul assured us through his letter to the believers in Philippi that "He who has begun a good work in you will complete it until the day of Jesus Christ" (Philippians 1:6). But Paul continued to encourage them in that letter to "work out your own salvation with fear and trembling" (Philippians 2:12). Wait—what?! He will do the work, but I've also gotta work? Yes. It's a beautiful tension. We work hard as we rest in Him. We walk obediently in what God asks of us, and we depend on His strength to do it, not our own. That means that we do have a responsibility to live a life that points to and is all about Jesus—but God equips us to do that work. He gives us the strength and joy and grace to live faithfully. As I offer myself to God and obey Him, I have the confidence that I will be transformed to look more and more like Christ. Then and only then will I be able to accomplish what He asks me to do.

When it comes to meal planning and journaling, I'm working on it! But when it comes to salvation and sanctification—being made new in Jesus—I can be a good finisher because I serve the God who always finishes what He starts.

INVITING THE LORD'S PRESENCE INTO THIS MOMENT

Father, thank You that I can be fully confident that You are faithful to finish what You've started in me. I am depending on You to transform me more and more into the one You've made me to be. Today, show me the areas of my life where You are at work in me, and give me the flexibility and grace to move and flow with You. Amen.

HEALTHY HEART

O LORD, You have searched me and known me.
You know my sitting down and my rising up;
You understand my thought afar off.
You comprehend my path and my lying down,
And are acquainted with all my ways.

PSALM 139:1–3

God, I want more of You, but I can't go further up and further in with a stinky attitude. My heart is the issue, and I know that I have severe heart issues. I can be so nasty on the inside, and I have so much attitude on the outside. Lord, I am so sorry. I need You to change it—change me—as only You can. Amen.

I HAD MY YEARLY HEALTH CHECKUP along with some medical testing done recently, and I discovered that everything looked healthy. I was glad for the good report, and I was especially relieved to know that my heart was just fine.

How helpful would it be if we could use a similar diagnostic tool to find out how our heart is doing *spiritually*? To get a blood sample, have some scans, and see exactly what is going on "under the hood" of our hearts?

It can be tricky because—from the outside—we can appear as if we have it all together and that our heart is doing "just fine." We worship with the church regularly. We spend time reading our Bibles. We volunteer and serve and sacrifice. We pray. We encourage others. We can be doing all the right things, saying all the right things, yet there can still be a disconnect between our heart and our life.

I want to suggest that there actually *is* a test we can take. In Psalm 139, we get to listen in as David speaks to God. He begins by acknowledging that God has searched him and knows him. It's like he's giving God an all-access backstage pass to the depths of his soul as he seeks God's leadership and guidance for his life.

We might be able to hide from people at church or work or school, or from our friends. It's possible even to hide what's in our hearts from the people who live under our roof. But there is no hiding from God. How did that work for Adam and Eve in the garden after they sinned? They tried to hide, but they couldn't. God's not the best one to play hide-and-seek with.

We desperately need this kind of deep heart check—*and* it's possible. We can't go to our family practitioner for an easy test and immediate results, but we *can* go to *the* Doctor, *the* Healer, and invite Him into the heart check, and even the surgery, we need. But I do need to warn you: When you ask God to search you and know you, He will take you up on it. And it's usually not pretty or comfortable. It's generally tough to see what's really going on, like when you smell that smell coming from the oven while it's preheating and you look in and realize this thing hasn't been cleaned since possibly ever. The One who knows you intimately can, and will, identify the places inside you that need to be cleansed and healed. You just have to give Him access. And the result? A healthy spiritual heart that overflows into an abundant, Christ-centered life.

INVITING THE LORD'S PRESENCE INTO THIS MOMENT

Ready your heart and ask God to search it. A little pre-op, so to speak. Read Psalm 139 and assume the humble posture of David. Open up your life to God. Surrender to His capable hands, and let Him in. Allow Him to speak, and then let your heart and soul and mind experience His loving-kindness in the morning, telling Him to have His way in your life.

CALLED TO KALISPELL?!

Give us help from trouble,
For the help of man is useless.
Through God we will do valiantly,
For it is He who shall tread down our enemies.

PSALM 108:12–13

Lord, You know all things, and You know where, when, and how. Forgive me for my attitude as I've let the stress and emotions get to me. Change my heart, O God! Lord, have Your way in me, right where You've planted me. Show me what to do. Show me how. Lord, teach me to trust in You. Help me today to seek You first. Amen.

When God began to stir our hearts about making a big move, we never thought it would be to Montana, let alone to a little city called Kalispell. We had always felt a call to start a church in a big city, because we felt like God was calling us to reach a lot of people. And here He was, leading us to the wilderness, where there *weren't* a lot of people. But there was lots of room to trust God.

We visited the week of Thanksgiving, and we arrived with a lot of questions, but we also came just to see and receive what God might be leading us into. My prayer that week was simple: *Lord, You know all things, and You know where, when, and how. Show us.*

What I *did* know was that anything we'd accomplish in ministry—whether we stayed put or whether we moved on to whatever God had next for us—would not be by our own will, or might, or gifts, or efforts. That weekend we prayed, "Give us help from trouble, for the help of man is useless. Through God we will do valiantly, for it is He who shall tread down our enemies" (Psalm 108:12–13).

From the moment I met Levi I could see that God's hand was on him and that He had great things in store for his life. Could this greatness be cultivated in Kalispell? As we prayed, as Levi sought counsel from his dad, and as we discussed our calling with others we trusted, it felt like a big leap of faith to trust God by following Him to Kalispell. To say yes to a call in this quaint town in northwestern Montana required us to fully surrender our goals. Our dreams. Our lives. I knew beyond a shadow of a doubt that God had a great calling on Levi's life to preach the gospel and to lead. Was this *that*?

Today—almost twenty years later—I can answer that question with a resounding yes! But in that moment, our human help—despite the best counsel—was worthless. God would have to provide the victory, which He has, in every single way.

I don't know what your "Kalispell" is today. Maybe, like us, it's a move. Or it might be a proposal. An adoption. An adventure. An entrepreneurial step. Or even the faith to stay put. No matter how unlikely it seems, saying yes to God's unlikely plan for you will be worth it. You never know what a simple yes to God will unlock in your life.

YOU NEVER KNOW WHAT A SIMPLE YES TO GOD WILL UNLOCK IN YOUR LIFE.

INVITING THE LORD'S PRESENCE INTO THIS MOMENT

When we can't quite see all that God can see, it can be hard to say yes. It can be hard to take that step that He's leading us to. What in your life today requires you to trust God whether you can see it or not? Take some time renewing your trust in the God who created the universe. Ask Him to help you see the next step. Ask Him for the courage to freshly surrender into His hands, His plan, and His will, and then ask Him to help you obey Him.

Fresh Mercy #4

BECOMING MORE LIKE JESUS

I HAVE THE CHOICE TO REJOICE

The LORD is my strength and my shield;
My heart trusted in Him, and I am helped;
Therefore my heart greatly rejoices,
And with my song I will praise Him.

PSALM 28:7

Lord God, thank You for holding this year in Your hands and for being in control of it all. Thank You for being my strength and my shield. Help me to be more resilient and kind, and help me to greatly rejoice in You. I want to go deeper. Take me there, to the place where You are. Amen.

HAVE YOU EVER CHOSEN—OR BEEN given—a *word* for the year? Maybe at the beginning of January, or on your birthday? I've known people who dedicate an entire year to *peace* or *kindness* or *gratitude*.

This has actually been a really fruitful rhythm in my own life. During my twenty-seventh year, I camped out in Psalm 27. So as twenty-eight approached, I asked God to give me a vision for the next year of my life. I spent time asking God to show me what He wanted to do *in me* over that year.

Well, it was almost like God was just *waiting* for me to ask, because what He gave me was quick and clear, from Psalm 28: "The LORD is my strength and my shield; my heart trusted in Him, and I am helped; therefore my heart greatly rejoices, and with my song I will praise Him" (v. 7). The phrase I knew was for me was "my heart greatly rejoices."

I'll confess: It's easy for me to wake up in the morning ready to praise and declare, "Good morning, Lord!" while reading my Bible and spending time with Jesus, with some coffee or tea in hand. But too often, as the day

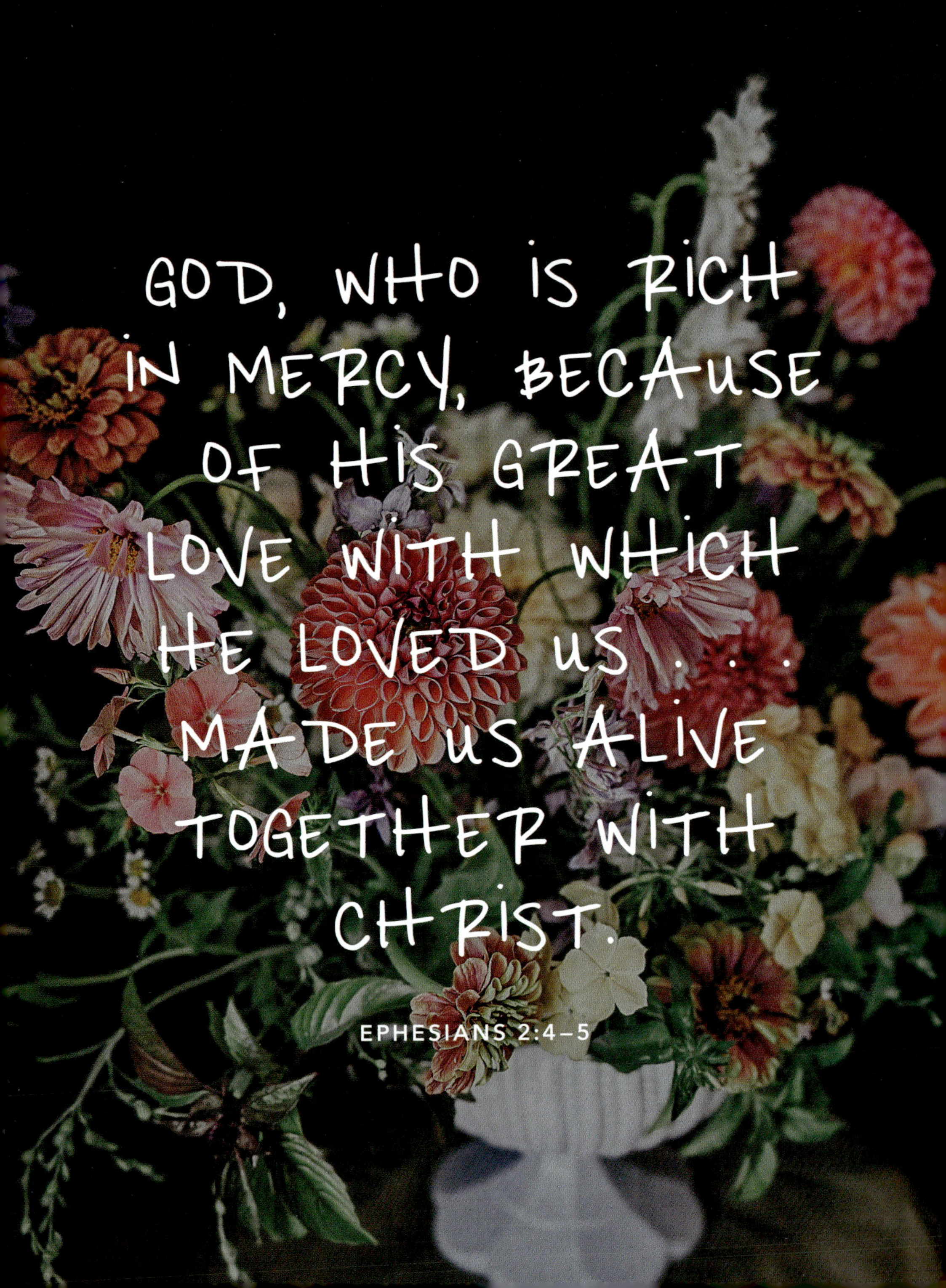

God, who is rich in mercy, because of His great love with which He loved us . . . made us alive together with Christ.

Ephesians 2:4–5

progresses, I can be quick to let situations or people steal my joy. I tend to let interruptions to my plans for the day take me down. I start off kind and patient and loving, and suddenly I find myself on my own personal struggle bus, reacting and ready to fight. I can be slow to forgive. I want to worship God wherever I am, because praise can get me out of the pits I so easily fall into. But to do this, I have to stop, take a breath, take a moment, and remember who my strength is: the Lord. I need to remember who my shield is: the Lord. And I need to recalibrate and worship in the middle of the War of the Daily Things.

It's been a minute since I was twenty-eight. In that year, God did a deep work in my heart to transform me with the word *rejoice.* And that work is ongoing—always. I still ask God to be my strength and shield, and to help me trust Him so that my heart can truly rejoice and I can praise Him with all that I am.

INVITING THE LORD'S PRESENCE INTO THIS MOMENT

If you struggle to rejoice as I have, I want you to be kind to yourself in this area. Every day we face challenges of many kinds, and I'll be the first to tell you that it doesn't *feel* natural to rejoice in the midst of the mess. This is exactly why we need God's help. We need help to look up. Make some space today and ask God to help you rejoice. Or even just try to say out loud, "I praise You, God. I don't understand, but I praise You. I don't like this, but I worship You." Watch as He changes your perspective and opens your eyes to see purpose and power in the very places where you once saw only pain.

GORGEOUS SKIN, BUT . . .

Whom have I in heaven but You?
And there is none upon earth that I desire besides You.
My flesh and my heart fail;
But God is the strength of my heart and my portion forever.

PSALM 73:25–26

Lord God, help me today to see what is unseen and, by faith, to see You working in the light affliction I face now for Your glory and for that which has eternal value. Take my eyes off what is temporal and give me eyes to see what lasts forever. Amen.

YOUR SKIN IS GORGEOUS, BUT don't rest on your laurels."

My new dermatologist had just finished inspecting almost every square inch of my skin. His comment at once delighted me and also felt like a punch right in the gut.

He continued, "You've been doing a great job taking care of your skin, and don't stop. But remember that a day is coming when it really won't matter what you've done to take care of your skin, because saggy, sun-damaged skin is coming for us all."

It stings, man! But true. Too true.

As I drove home from the clinic, I continued to reflect on his words. In fact, they reminded me of Levi's sermon series titled "You in Five Years." In it, he invited us to be intentional in the choices we were currently making, considering who we wanted to be in the future. Specifically, he was

MY FLESH AND
MY HEART FAIL;
BUT GOD IS
THE STRENGTH
OF MY HEART
AND MY PORTION
FOREVER.
PSALM 73:26

challenging our church to consider how the small things we were doing in the present could change the trajectory of our lives.

In one message, my husband actually mentioned a skin-care study that had been recently conducted. Half of those who were studied applied sunscreen every day, and the other half applied sunscreen only when they felt they "needed" it. The photos he shared of the two groups, after decades of this practice, instilled a deep fear in me of the choices I'd been making, making me want to do my best with what I've got.

In 2 Corinthians 4:16, Paul admonished, "Therefore we do not lose heart. Even though our outward man is perishing, yet the inward man is being renewed day by day." In previous verses, Paul had been talking about the beating that our bodies can take as we live this life surrendered to Christ, "always carrying about in the body the dying of the Lord Jesus, that the life of Jesus also may be manifested in our body" (v. 10). Living our lives for His glory and His name can bring wounds and scars and a weight that our bodies will always keep score of. Yes, this includes old age—and the ailments and aches and pains that go along with it—but Paul's reminder is life-changing and mind-shifting: *We do not lose heart.* Even when the youth and tight skin we once possessed fade. Even though we start experiencing aches and bruises that seem to come out of nowhere. Even when the diagnosis we never thought would come is now in our story, the good news is that in Christ, our inward person, who we truly are, is being renewed and strengthened every day. It is being empowered to continue serving God until the day we see Him face-to-face—in our resurrected bodies, which won't ever break down. Best news ever!

Beautiful friend, although your flesh and your heart may fail, you can confidently declare that God is the strength of your heart and your portion forever. And that's something to rejoice about—and share with others!

INVITING THE LORD'S PRESENCE INTO THIS MOMENT

Read Psalm 73:25–28 in ***The Message*****:**

> You're all I want in heaven!
> You're all I want on earth!
> When my skin sags and my bones get brittle,
> God is rock-firm and faithful.
> Look! Those who left you are falling apart!
> Deserters, they'll never be heard from again.
> But I'm in the very presence of God—
> oh, how refreshing it is!
> I've made Lord God my home.
> God, I'm telling the world what you do!

What leaps from this version into your heart? Linger in that. Ask God for a deeper desperation for more of Him and His presence in your everyday life. Start with today.

ISN'T SHE LOVELY?

Strength and honor are her clothing;
She shall rejoice in time to come.
She opens her mouth with wisdom,
And on her tongue is the law of kindness.
She watches over the ways of her household,
And does not eat the bread of idleness.

PROVERBS 31:25–27

My Lord, my Love, the Man of my life, thank You for creating me and designing me to be Your daughter. I am Yours first and foremost, and I want to walk with You so closely that it becomes completely clear what it means to be Your daughter: a woman, a brave and kind leader, and a tender, compassionate, courageous lady. Amen.

One day I went into a public ladies' restroom and saw this written in white paint on the door:

lady [ˈlā-dē] *noun*. A woman who is refined, polite, and well-spoken.

I had not expected to be inspired in a public restroom that day, but it was right at a moment in my life, in my day, when I really needed the reminder of who God had made me to be. It was a moment when I needed a nudge from my heavenly Father. And in the way only God can, He used the graffiti on a bathroom door to remind me of the true, beautiful, warm lady He had designed me to be.

I needed it because there are times when I get so overwhelmed by what's happening around me and the hard things in my life that I forget who I am. When that happens, I'll need the reminder that God has made me to bring His love and kindness into each situation I'll face—no matter how small it might be. And on that day, visiting that restroom was my moment to pause, rest, think, and pray. As I washed my hands, I asked God to help me be this kind of woman.

THERE ARE TIMES WHEN I GET SO OVERWHELMED BY WHAT'S HAPPENING AROUND ME . . . THAT I FORGET WHO I AM.

Have you ever had some kind of reminder (as random as it might have been) that invited you to live in the fullness of how God designed you? Maybe you ran into an old friend who knew you when your spirit was softer and more pliable to the things of God. Or maybe you met up with a mentor whose gracious heart inspired you to want to be kinder. Or maybe you've caught a glimpse in Scripture of what it looks like to be lovely.

I'm thankful for these reminders that God so kindly—and usually humorously—gives me. I need them. I need Him. And I am confident that He is strengthening and growing me into the person I'm meant to be—more and more like Jesus—until I get to see Him face-to-face in heaven and am perfectly pure in His presence. And I'm confident in this very thing for you too: His mercy and joy *over* you, *in* you, and *through* you and your words to others.

INVITING THE LORD'S PRESENCE INTO THIS MOMENT

Take a moment and consider the woman God created you to be. Maybe you feel further from her today than you used to be, or maybe you feel closer to her. Ask God to give you a greater glimpse into this woman who is you. Reflect on Proverbs 31:25–27 and invite God to show you what those words mean *for you.* Isn't she lovely? How does He want to strengthen you on the inside? How does He want to grow you in being able to laugh and find beauty and humor in the little things? How is He prompting you to speak up and use your words to speak life and peace and joy over yourself and others? You are lovely.

DECORATING THE INTERIOR

Finally, brethren, whatever things are true, whatever things are noble, whatever things are just, whatever things are pure, whatever things are lovely, whatever things are of good report, if there is any virtue and if there is anything praiseworthy—meditate on these things.

PHILIPPIANS 4:8

Lord, I commit my mind and thoughts to You. I look to You to make me more like Jesus and to make me more into the person You've created me to be. Today, deepen my relationship with You. Amen.

FAMILY
SECRET

MY FAVORITE DRINK FOR MOST of my preteen and teenage years was Snapple—especially the Peach Tea, Mango Madness, and Kiwi Strawberry flavors. Back in the day (the 1990s, to be more specific), Snapple came in a glass bottle and had a paper label wrapped around it. I would take off the label, cut the pretty part off, and then decorate my bedroom wall with it. Over time, I had created a wall full of this "Snapple wallpaper." I also painted another wall by cutting sponges and dipping them into paint to give the wall texture. It was my beautiful, creative mess, and I loved it. I was so thankful for the freedom my mom gave me to be artistic with my walls.

I have always loved interior decorating. Ever since I was little, it's been a passion of mine to decorate and rearrange—and then redecorate and re-rearrange—using unlikely items to brighten up my walls and make my room feel fresh. A few years ago, I met a professional interior designer who was incredible. First of all, her vibe was so cool. She was Asian with a slicked-back low bun, beautiful skin with not a lot of makeup, and black, thick-framed glasses. She had a simple and comfortable—yet elegant—way about her. Before I even knew she was a professional interior designer, I thought, *I want to be like her when I grow up!* (At least I already had the Asian part going for me!) She told me that although she'd never gone to college, she'd learned what she could from others and kept practicing. She encouraged me, saying, "If it's a passion of yours, just keep learning and growing in it. Keep practicing, and then keep going." Over the years, I've done that—just not any of the "professional" part.

What about you? While designing the interior of your home may or may not be as life-giving for you as it is for me, each of us has an "interior" in need of attention and care. I believe we alone are responsible for the condition of our own interiors: our hearts. Take a moment and imagine the atmosphere in your heart. When we consider the condition of our hearts, it can be measured by our thoughts. They are what determine the interior life within us.

And just like I've chosen the colors and patterns and designs for the walls of my physical home, we also choose the thoughts that occupy our hearts. When it comes to our own interior, the apostle Paul exhorted us to choose what is true and noble and right and pure and lovely and admirable. He encouraged us to think about anything that is excellent or praiseworthy. That's what makes for a beautiful heart. I encourage you to embrace the job of interior designer of your soul and of the condition of your heart by choosing to think the kind of thoughts that will beautify the atmosphere of your heart for His glory.

INVITING THE LORD'S PRESENCE INTO THIS MOMENT

Lord, as I commit my mind and thoughts to You, open my eyes to see the interior of my heart. Help me to choose the truth when it would be easier to believe the lies. Help me to choose the pure when it would be easy to go the impure route. Help me to practice choosing Your way in the little things, so I will build my muscle memory to choose faith over fear. I choose right now to be still and sit in Your presence. I choose to lift my eyes. I choose to let my roots go even deeper in You. Amen.

HE MAKES EVERYTHING BEAUTIFUL

He has made everything beautiful in its time. Also He has put eternity in their hearts, except that no one can find out the work that God does from beginning to end.

ECCLESIASTES 3:11

Lord, I am eager to display Your beauty, so I welcome You to be at work in my life. I confess that I often feel like a bundle of sticks and leaves. I invite You to work in my heart and make me new. Amen.

A love language of mine is flowers.

And I don't even mean that someone has to give me flowers. I am delighted just being in the presence of flowers. Maybe I'm picking them. Or I could be creating a wildflower arrangement (usually with my daughter Daisy—we share this love of wildflowers). Perhaps one of my kids has just given me a little dandelion bouquet. Flowers bring me such joy.

When Levi and I were first married, I loved flowers, but I didn't feel like I was a "store-bought bouquet" kind of girl. My wedding bouquet had been mostly made up of large green leaves and a few calla lilies. I decorated each table at the reception with a bamboo plant set in a cup or vase I'd found at a thrift store. And I have a distinct memory from those early days of telling Levi that I didn't need him to buy me flowers. And at the time, I meant it.

But a few years ago, I mentioned to him that I really *would* love to receive flowers. I think the conversation might have actually turned into a fight, and I told him, "It could just be a handful of wildflowers you picked. But it would *show* me that you're thinking of me!"

Yeah, that's right. I can be real fun.

If you've watched any DIY videos showing how to make an arrangement of flowers, you know that it always begins pretty—stark. What's deposited first in the vase are the sticks. The greenery. The non-blooming participants in a collection of beauties. At the beginning, it doesn't look particularly *flowery*. But then the florist, or "flower stylist," begins adding the blooms, and soon the whole bouquet begins to make more sense and becomes more beautiful.

Isn't this how God works? He begins a work in us. He starts with something brown or green, but there's no real color yet. It doesn't make sense yet. But then He adds in a small flower. There's a pop of color. And then He gets on a roll and adds in more and more exotic and stunning blooms.

DEAR HEART, THE LORD IS WORKING IN YOU.

Dear heart, the Lord is working in you—in His timing. You might feel like your life is just a bundle of sticks and leaves and nothing worthy of becoming a stunning arrangement, but the story of your life is what He's writing and continuing to write. So let Him. Trust Him. You're in the safe, creative, and loving hands of *the* Gardener.

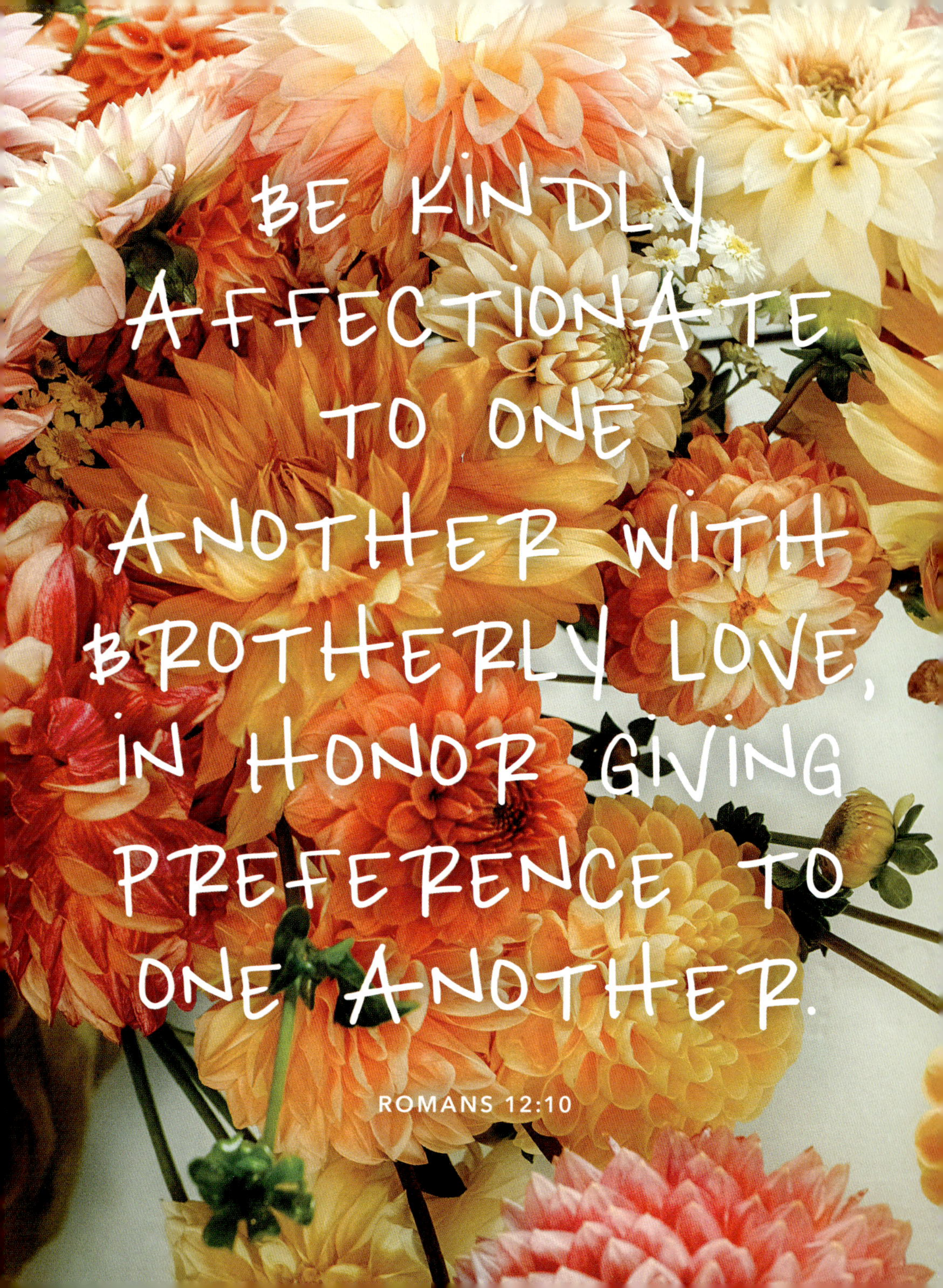
BE KINDLY
AFFECTIONATE
TO ONE
ANOTHER WITH
BROTHERLY LOVE,
IN HONOR GIVING
PREFERENCE TO
ONE ANOTHER.
ROMANS 12:10

INVITING THE LORD'S PRESENCE INTO THIS MOMENT

When was that season (possibly today!) when your life looked like a bundle of dry sticks? Can you remember a barren time when you couldn't see the work God was doing in you yet? Take some time to remember those seasons and notice what beauty God eventually created in and through them. Surrender your timing to Him, and invite His way and His timing into your heart. Rest. He makes everything beautiful in His time.

BROTHERS AND SISTERS AND OTHERS

Be kindly affectionate to one another with brotherly love, in honor giving preference to one another; not lagging in diligence, fervent in spirit, serving the Lord; rejoicing in hope, patient in tribulation, continuing steadfastly in prayer; distributing to the needs of the saints, given to hospitality.

ROMANS 12:10–13

Lord, teach me how to love my brothers and sisters. Let there be purity, kindness, patience, and peace in our interactions. Help me to receive Your love in a fresh way today so that I can let it flow to the others in my life, especially the ones who are more difficult to love. Amen.

When my little brother Ryan and I were growing up, there was a good deal of joking and poking and mocking and jabbing. (I see a very similar dynamic between my son and the sister who is closest to him in age.) Being two and a half years older than Ryan, I was taller and stronger than him—but only for a short while. One day, everything changed. I gave Ryan a little jab, and when he pushed me back, I really felt it. I quickly realized that he had grown stronger than me and was now able to hurt me. So I backed off.

While Ryan could still pound me with one punch today, I am thankful that our relationship has matured into friendship. The apostle Paul counseled those in the early church to "be kindly affectionate to one another with brotherly love" (Romans 12:10). The Greek word he used for "love" is *philadelphia*—a brotherly love. Paul encouraged the church in Rome to be kind, to be affectionate, and to give preference to one another. He was encouraging the care and keeping and loving of one another in the body of Christ. The *type* of care he's inviting Christians into is marked by awareness, kindness, honor, diligence, rejoicing, and patience.

When you pull apart the word *brother*, you find that the word *other* is

PAUL ENCOURAGED THE CHURCH IN ROME TO BE KIND, TO BE AFFECTIONATE, AND TO GIVE PREFERENCE TO ONE ANOTHER.

tucked inside. The wordplay can be a reminder that a central tenet of being a Christian hinges on how we interact with the "others" in our lives. Sometimes those others are the actual siblings we grew up with. Other times it will be our brothers and sisters in the church. And throughout the ministry of Jesus, we see how He honored and engaged with really surprising "others," like women, tax collectors, and fishermen—all the unlikely crew members we find Him with in the Gospels.

Who are the "others" that you're being called to love with kindness and brotherly affection today?

INVITING THE LORD'S PRESENCE INTO THIS MOMENT

Spend some time praying for the "others" in your life today. Out of those you will interact with today, who is the most difficult for you to love? Jesus loved the unlovable and the untouchable. Ask Him for a refreshed heart when it comes to the people in your life. You have been put in their circle for a reason. Ask Him to help you see it and to boldly walk in all He asks of you today when it comes to loving, leading, helping, and serving others. He will give you everything you need, and He will give you His love, especially when you feel like you have nothing left to give. Lean in to His love for you and for others today.

LIVING IN THE FRESH

Therefore, if anyone is in Christ, he is a new creation; old things have passed away; behold, all things have become new. Now all things are of God, who has reconciled us to Himself through Jesus Christ, and has given us the ministry of reconciliation.

2 CORINTHIANS 5:17–18

Lord, I believe You when You say that I am in You and I am a new creation. But would You help me to live this out today? Remind me that I belong to You and that I have been made clean and righteous only because of You. Open my eyes today, and may my life show how much I'm in love with You. Amen.

WHEN LEVI AND I HAD been married just two and a half months, we co-led a mission trip to Macedonia. Talk about trial by fire! It felt really hard—because it was!

When we got home, I unpacked the experience in my journal:

This was an intense trip. I feel like I learned so much but at the same time, I feel like I failed at being a co-leader and a wife. I was so overwhelmingly bombarded by lies from the Enemy that I was often tempted to believe I was weak. I was tempted daily to believe the lies that I'm worthless and a failure and that I have no gifts. I felt like I was "good for nothing."

Pretty rough, huh? It really was. The struggle with insecurity is so real for me!

And yet I know that every one of us can be tempted to believe the lies of the deceiver about who we are. The enemy finds our weak spots, those places in our lives that confirm the accusations of the one who lies, and then he whispers:

You're not smart enough.
You're not pretty enough.
You're not spiritual enough.
You're not strong enough.
You're simply not enough.

When you find yourself tangled up in that trap, I hope you remember that you are not alone. You can ask God to help you stand in what is most true. But also? I know how you feel, along with every other woman in all of history. It's just the truth.

When I literally cried to the Lord to help me, He reminded me of Paul's words in his second letter to the church in Corinth: "Therefore, if anyone is in Christ, he is a new creation; old things have passed away; behold, all things have become new" (2 Corinthians 5:17). God also spoke through the word of a pastor's wife I met in Macedonia, who encouraged me, saying, "Don't let in any guilt, because it will only hurt you." She also directed me back to the truth of Scripture.

Sweet friend, we have a real enemy who seeks to harm us by planting thoughts of shame and guilt in our minds. But it's possible to keep them from taking root in our hearts when we choose to stand on the truth that we are made *new* in Christ. We get to live with a newness and a freshness that we can't get anywhere else.

INVITING THE LORD'S PRESENCE INTO THIS MOMENT

Guilt and shame can easily become our go-to. If this has been your perpetual old way of thinking, then turning your back on it can be really difficult. Being open about your struggles with trusted friends, pastors, leaders, or counselors is definitely a good place to start. But it's also so important to keep reminding yourself of who you are in Christ—a new creation. It's true that you are a new creation that still deals with the old self. It's a daily tension, a daily fight. But the *reality* is that you are a new creation. So today, let this truth be infused into your mind, your heart, your body. Let Him renew you today. Let Him refresh your spirit. Ask the Lord how He wants to build something in you fresh today. It's a process, and sometimes it feels really slow, but He's faithfully working in you. Run to Him in this moment. He's right there.

POTHOLES AND PITFALLS, A.K.A. PARENTING

Train up a child in the way he should go,
And when he is old he will not depart from it.

PROVERBS 22:6

Lord, help me today to navigate the rocky road of parenting with Your grace and Your love in the driver's seat. Help me to approach my children and the other children in my life with Your tenderness and vision for their lives. Let me remember today how it feels to be secure in Your love, cared for by You, and known by You, and let me carefully care for the little hearts that You let me love in that same way. Amen.

Most days when I'm in our family-sized car, I'm taking a child to tennis, to a piano lesson, or to church or youth group. Very rarely do I drive alone.

And yet one day I did find myself driving alone, and I started to pay attention to the actual Montana road I was driving on. Some patches were only gravel. Some areas had a little ditch in the road, and in other spots there were large potholes. Sometimes small branches or larger limbs had fallen in the way. And there would even be the occasional chipmunk or deer leaping across the road. It's real, guys.

On this particular day, driving alone in

silence, I was praying for my children. I was asking God for help in understanding them, teaching them, and training them—and each in their own unique way (which can itself be overwhelming). But then, as I was navigating slowly around a few huge potholes in the same area, I felt like God impressed on my heart, *This is how I want you to approach parenting.*

It seemed like God was opening my eyes to not speed over the precarious or dangerous spots in the road I was traveling while parenting our children. Instead, I needed to slow down. To take care. To pay attention. To anticipate the bumps. He prompted me to watch closely and respond thoughtfully. And with a deep breath, I received it.

I FELT LIKE GOD IMPRESSED ON MY HEART, THIS IS HOW I WANT YOU TO APPROACH PARENTING.

The author of Proverbs coached parents, "Train up a child in the way he should go, and when he is old he will not depart from it" (22:6). What I believe God was teaching me that day while driving was the necessity of paying attention and trusting Him as I navigated the particular terrain of each child, in each situation. It is definitely a daily trust, a daily training, and a daily reminder to be patient with our kids the way God is with us.

It is a good word, both for parenting children and for navigating all kinds of relationships. Whether you're struggling to navigate family relationships, or ones with friends or colleagues or enemies, God is so *faithful* to guide you and lead you in the way you should go. Allow God to keep giving you a teachable spirit so you can receive the training in your own life, and keep asking Him to give you the necessary care and humility to be able to train those He's given you.

INVITING THE LORD'S PRESENCE INTO THIS MOMENT

God is faithful to train us as His children. He is also our Shepherd, and He sees our journey from beginning to end. If you have children, you know the daily dependence on Jesus that you need in order to parent and train your kids. If you are a teacher, youth leader, aunt, or grandmother, you have a unique voice in the lives of the young hearts around you too. Whatever your role, God will be faithful to lead you as you lead them. So lean in to His leadership. Lean in to His shepherding. Spend time pressing into His presence. The Holy Spirit will guide you. Ask Him. Trust Him today.

Fresh Mercy #5

BELIEVING GOD WHEN IT DOESN'T MAKE SENSE

WHAT TO DO ON "ONE OF THOSE DAYS"

Now David was greatly distressed, for the people spoke of stoning him, because the soul of all the people was grieved, every man for his sons and his daughters. But David strengthened himself in the LORD his God.

1 SAMUEL 30:6

Father, I turn to You. Today I feel frazzled. Undone. Distressed. You know my heart, and You know that I need You. I can't face this day alone. Teach me to find my strength and grace in You. Amen.

JUST AS I WAS GETTING into bed, I found the biggest bruise on my knee that I had ever had—ever. I gasped, and Levi asked what was wrong. "I have no idea how I got this bruise—it's the biggest one I've ever had in my life!"

Ever have one of those days? You get to the end of the day and look back, wondering what you did or how things happened without your even knowing it. Maybe you just felt behind all day. You wonder what you accomplished, if anything at all. You just want to go to bed so you can start fresh in the morning, bruises and all.

Some days are just rough. Other days feel even more brutal. Like when we are given a diagnosis. Or we discover an infidelity. Or we receive news of the death of someone we love so very much.

What do you do with your bad day?

In 1 Samuel 30, David had a *really* bad day. He returned from battle to the town where he lived, only to find that his enemies had burned it down and taken his family captive. Verse 6 says that David was greatly distressed, which is no surprise, since David and his men were grieving the loss of their wives and children.

"But David strengthened himself in the LORD his God" (1 Samuel 30:6).

The Bible doesn't say *exactly* how David strengthened himself in the Lord. But we know that throughout the psalms he authored, he was honest with God. He grieved and cried out to the Lord. In Psalm 143, for example, he said things like, "Hear my prayer, O LORD" (v. 1), "For the enemy has persecuted my soul; he has crushed my life to the ground" (v. 3), "Answer me speedily, O LORD; my spirit fails!" (v. 7), and "Deliver me, O LORD, from my enemies; in You I take shelter. Teach me to do Your will, for You are my God; Your Spirit is good" (vv. 9–10). David proved time and time again, in psalm after psalm, that the way through a particularly bad day is by engaging in prayer, praise, and a posture of humility. He ended Psalm 143 declaring, "For I am Your servant" (v. 12). From the times when David was shepherding his father's sheep in the wilderness to his time as king, we witness his bent toward praise. He worshipped in the worry. He prayed in the pain. He humbled himself before his holy God.

So what kind of bad day—or week, or year, or season—have you recently experienced?

Whatever you're facing, be honest with God. He can handle it. Are you angry? Are you hurt? Are you disappointed? Are you grieving? Strengthen yourself in the Lord like David did. Tell God about it. Ask for His perspective. Ask Him to help you see what you're facing through the lens of faith. It stings, but the Lord will strengthen you.

THE LORD IS NEAR TO THOSE WHO HAVE A BROKEN HEART, AND SAVES SUCH AS HAVE A CONTRITE SPIRIT.

PSALM 34:18

INVITING THE LORD'S PRESENCE INTO THIS MOMENT

If you feel like you don't even have the *strength* to strengthen yourself in the Lord, that's the perfect place to be. The Lord invites you right now to come to Him just as you are. Psalm 143:6 says, "I spread out my hands to You; my soul longs for You like a thirsty land." Sometimes it's hard to form words as we pray to God. If that's the case for you, consider kneeling before Him. Consider spreading your arms out to Him, telling Him with your physical posture that your soul thirsts and longs for Him. And then you could even pray like David did in verse 8: "Cause me to hear Your lovingkindness in the morning, for in You do I trust; cause me to know the way in which I should walk, for I lift up my soul to You." Let David's prayer become your own and see how God meets you right where you are.

FRESH STARTS

And He said to me, "My grace is sufficient for you, for My strength is made perfect in weakness." Therefore most gladly I will rather boast in my infirmities, that the power of Christ may rest upon me. Therefore I take pleasure in infirmities, in reproaches, in needs, in persecutions, in distresses, for Christ's sake. For when I am weak, then I am strong.

2 CORINTHIANS 12:9–10

Lord, thank You for this new day. Thank You that Your mercies are brand-new this morning. Thank You for being the God of fresh starts, of new beginnings, of second chances. You are continually gracious, tenderly extending mercy and kindness. You are God, and You are good. Your mercy endures forever. Amen.

I'VE GOT PUFFY EYES, WORN out from long days and late nights. I was cranky with my kids as we did our homeschool lessons today. This week I've not been the most encouraging wife. And guess what I'm supposed to do this weekend? I'm scheduled to speak to and encourage the moms in our church. (*Really, Lord?! Are You kidding me right now?!*) The irony of me being a sorry soul who's about to "encourage" other moms right now feels like a bad joke and a nightmare all at once.

Taking a deep breath at the kitchen sink, I close my eyes and pray, *Father, give me the words to say. What should I even talk about?*

I mess up—with my family, in my walk with Jesus, in my self-discipline—a lot. But it's also important for me to name it here so you know you're not alone.

I wrestle to love and honor my husband.

I struggle to love, train, and teach my kids.

I fail to be the kind of human God designed me to be.

I ache with shame and regret and disappointment.

I am slow to run to Jesus when I need Him most.

Truly, I'm a hot mess (although my husband sweetly says, "With the emphasis on *hot*, and you might be a mess, but you're *my* mess"—thanks, my love). And yet . . . the Bible shows us imperfect human after imperfect human who God desired to use, and *did use*, to build His kingdom—right in the midst of their brokenness. Despite their flaws and mess-ups and sins. I'm so grateful that I'm not alone, *and* that we serve a God who can take ashes and bring beauty from them.

I'M SO GRATEFUL THAT I'M NOT ALONE, AND THAT WE SERVE A GOD WHO CAN TAKE ASHES AND BRING BEAUTY FROM THEM.

In the midst of my messes, I can see them as extra opportunities to depend on God. Instead of feeling overcome with guilt and shame, I can practice praying:

I'm sorry, Lord, I messed that one up again.

I have no idea what I'm doing, and I really need You right now.

Help me lead people when I'm still learning what it means and looks like to lead myself.

Help!

Dear friend, God's grace is sufficient. Whether you're dealing with things you've brought on yourself or aches and issues from others that God has allowed in your life, learn from Paul. He said he would rather boast in weakness, because then Christ's power would rest on him. What a promise for those of us who feel weak and *are* weak: When we are weak, then He is strong.

INVITING THE LORD'S PRESENCE INTO THIS MOMENT

You might be a hot mess, but imagine God telling you that you are *His* mess, and that He has plans for you in the midst of the mess. In the moments of frustration, when perhaps you feel like you should be further along than you are, have patience with yourself. Your God is a patient God. He's the One who began the work in you, and He will be faithful to complete it. Rest in His faithful work in you. Ask Him to help you see what He's specifically working on, and then join Him in it. Pray for growth, but also pray for an even more grateful heart—grateful for the fact that somehow, in His grace, His strength is made perfect in your weakness. When you are weak, His grace is sufficient for you. Receive it and run with it today!

WHEN YOUR DAUGHTER GETS TO HEAVEN BEFORE YOU

"Fear not, for I am with you;Be not dismayed, for I am your God.I will strengthen you,Yes, I will help you,I will uphold you with My righteous right hand."

ISAIAH 41:10

Lord, right now I'm achy and numb. It's been three weeks today since Lenya Avery went to heaven. I know that to God a thousand years is as a day, and a day is as a thousand years, but I wonder, What is time like in heaven?

OUR SECOND-BORN DAUGHTER, LENYA, WENT to heaven when she was five years old. She died of an asthma attack five days before Christmas, and as we headed into that next year, living it without her seemed inconceivable, impossible. Like any parent who has lost a child, I've wrestled to make sense of her life and our loss.

Still in shock, with a desperate aching in my soul, I was overwhelmed by emotions. I hated the thought of forgetting memories of the time we'd had. I was grateful for the five beautiful years we'd been given. There were moments of deep regret, which would bully me with thoughts that I should have been a better mother to her. I was comforted by the assurance that she was now in God's presence, experiencing fullness of joy.

In those days when our grief was palpable, my husband and I found that the only way through the pain was to feel it. In the moments of deep aching, I had to force myself to look up to the Lord; otherwise, the storm would inevitably knock me down and take me out (which also happened at times). God came close in that dark season in a way I had never experienced Him before. He poured out His love and His peace and His presence.

In his second letter to the church in Corinth, Paul wrote, "For our light affliction, which is but for a moment, is working for us a far more exceeding and eternal weight of glory" (4:17). And as God carried us through Lenya's death, this promise in God's Word became *real* to me. Somehow, by God's grace, I really did come to believe the truth that what we were enduring was actually momentary. Not only would our pain not last forever, but we had eternal glory to look forward to. In *The Message*, Eugene Peterson paraphrased Paul's words: "These hard times are small potatoes compared to the coming good times, the lavish celebration prepared for us" (2 Corinthians 4:17). The hard things we face in life are actually really hard. And they can be big. But when they're compared to the weight of eternal glory—compared to the lavish reality that heaven is—our grief is far outweighed. It doesn't make sense—at all. But that's part of this life of faith and hope and purpose that we get to live in right now. It's possible for you, too, dear one. Even here, He is near. Even here, He sees you and knows you and has a purpose of power in your pain.

HE SEES YOU AND KNOWS YOU AND HAS A PURPOSE OF POWER IN YOUR PAIN.

INVITING THE LORD'S PRESENCE INTO THIS MOMENT

Are you losing heart today? Or is someone in your life losing heart? You're in good company. Even Jesus begged His Father, in the garden of Gethsemane, to take away the cup of suffering that He was about to face. But then He said, "Not My will, but Yours, be done" (Luke 22:42).

He grieves with you and hates that you're experiencing this. But He also sees what this pain is producing in you, and in your friend who is hurting. Take a moment to surrender your pain to God. Take a moment and pray for the people in your life who are suffering. Ask God to help you fix your gaze on what is unseen, rather than what you see right now. Ask Him to strengthen your faith and to see this affliction for what it is—horrible, painful, traumatizing. But then again, for what it *really* is—light, momentary, and pointing to the eternal weight of glory.

DIS-ORDERED

If I must boast, I will boast in the things which concern my infirmity.

2 CORINTHIANS 11:30

Father, good morning. I'm having the hardest time praying right now. I'm getting so distracted with the most random things, and I lose track of my thoughts. Father, teach me to pray. Show me how to pray more effectively. Teach me how to trust You when I'm weak and distracted. Amen.

SEVERAL YEARS AGO, IN ONE particular session with my counselor, she began listing out some of the symptoms of PMDD (premenstrual dysphoric disorder). It's a severe form of PMS that includes intense emotional and physical symptoms—think cramps, but in your mind. At that time, I had never heard of it before. As she began telling me what the disorder looks like, dots across my whole life started connecting, making a lot of things make sense.

Before the light bulb came on for me during that conversation, there had been moments when I'd thought I was crazy. Quite literally. It felt particularly confusing because when I was good, I was *good*. But the lows, the pits, were *really bad*. Fights with my husband during this time of the month were consistent and traumatic—for me, for him, and for anyone within listening distance. In the midst of these storms, I felt like my whole life had exploded, and the bits and pieces would never be able to be gathered and put back together. I believed I was a bad wife, a bad mother, a bad friend, a bad daughter and sister, and a bad leader—just bad in general, and that something was deeply wrong with me. (And I also believed that my husband was horrible too.) And yet, after a few days had passed, the fog would lift. I'd feel "better," but then I'd be left with lingering remorse, shame, and frustration with myself.

Over the years, Levi and I have both learned—and are still learning—how to navigate these tricky moments. When I notice the symptoms coming on, I put myself in "time-out" (not in a mean way, but more in a "let me go over here for a minute" way) by taking a shower, taking some prescription medicine, or heading to bed. And, graciously, Levi will remind me, "Jennie, it's going to be okay. I love you, and you love me. Let's not make any huge decisions right now. Some of these things you've brought up are valid, but let's talk about them when the storm has receded a bit."

I have a feeling I will be learning and growing through this for the rest of my life, but I will say that I have already learned and grown so much when it comes to this disorder. I have learned that what I eat makes a big difference, and meeting with my doctor about my hormones has been huge. And remembering that this is part of my struggle and my story has helped me have more patience and grace with myself. I am learning what recharges me and what replenishes me, and also what depletes me. Like my husband says, it's not a problem to be solved but a tension to be managed. Once I realized I'm not doing it in my own strength but in His, and once I placed trusted people in my corner, it helped so much. And like Paul said, "If I must boast, I will boast in the things which concern my infirmity" (2 Corinthians 11:30). In my weakness, His strength is made known.

Surely goodness and mercy shall follow me all the days of my life; and I will dwell in the house of the Lord forever.

Psalm 23:6

If you suffer with anything similar, don't lose heart, sweet one. Keep showing up and learning. It will take hard work that you may not feel ready for or strong enough to do. Keep going. Lean into His love; there is hope there for you.

INVITING THE LORD'S PRESENCE INTO THIS MOMENT

Whether or not you suffer in the ways I do, take some time to notice the areas in your life where you are weak. They might be emotional and mental, like mine. They might be physical. They could be social. Spend some time offering God your weak places and consider what it means for Him to be *strong* in your weaknesses. Imagine Him sitting there with you, looking at you with love. You may not understand why He's allowed this, but you can be confident that He is with you every step of the way. Perhaps take some time to hold your hands out in front of you and release your worries about your weaknesses, and then receive His strength, His grace, and His mercy.

HE'S STILL THE ONE

The woman then left her waterpot, went her way into the city, and said to the men, "Come, see a Man who told me all things that I ever did. Could this be the Christ?"

JOHN 4:28–29

Lord, here I am. Thank You for meeting me and sending me. I am ready and willing for what You have asked of me. I am here for it, and I want to walk with You every day of my life, all the way to heaven, when I will see You face-to-face. Amen.

SOMETIMES WHEN WE READ ABOUT women and men in the Bible, we can be tempted to assume that they're *other* than we are. But when Jesus encountered a woman in Samaria, she was actually a lot like us.

Jesus was at the well in the middle of the day, long after all the other women had come and gone to collect their daily water. But if He had been there at a more reasonable time, before the most intense heat of the day, He would have missed the woman He needed to see. If you're not familiar with the passage, you should definitely read it. It's found in the fourth chapter of John's gospel, and it is stunning. (You should also watch the episode of *The Chosen* that depicts this scene—and be ready to weep.)

This woman likely came to the well at midday because she was an outcast. She had a reputation. To see Jesus as He spoke with her tenderly and to see her pure response to Him stops me in my tracks. Jesus talked with her about the life she had lived and was still living. He shared with her about the Living Water. And when He revealed His true identity to her, her eyes were opened. She left her water pot behind and ran to exclaim to the men in the city, "Come, see a Man who told me all things that I ever did. Could this be the Christ?" (John 4:29).

In this encounter, we see Jesus' heart for the outcast and those who feel left out. We listen in as He shared that He was the answer to the ache within her soul. This woman needed to know that she was seen by God, loved by Him, and called by Him. We see a beautiful change of countenance within this woman as a result of her encounter with Jesus. This woman, who hadn't had any hope, confidence, or voice, had suddenly found all three, and Jesus wanted her to be the first woman to proclaim His message, which she did when she ran to her village and asked, "Could this be the Christ?"

In the same way, Jesus is calling you to Himself today. He wants to speak to you and have a moment with you and remind you who you are. You are precious to Him. No matter what you've done, who you've been, or where you've gone, He wants you. He is the Living Water, and He will be the answer to your ache and thirst within. And not only does He want you—He also wants to move in you and through you.

What's your part? A willing heart, loyal to your Savior.

YOU ARE PRECIOUS TO HIM.

INVITING THE LORD'S PRESENCE INTO THIS MOMENT

One of the beautiful things about Jesus' encounter with this woman at the well was His radical knowledge and acceptance of her. Spend time receiving and reflecting on Jesus' intimate knowledge and acceptance of you. What are some of your thoughts about such a beautiful aspect of our God's character? In what ways are you noticing how He's inviting you to respond to this?

HE'S PREPARING YOU IN THIS VERY MOMENT

Then it came to pass, at the end of two full years, that Pharaoh had a dream; and behold, he stood by the river.

GENESIS 41:1

God, You know I need You. You know my heart, my mind, my worries, and my frustrations. You search me and know me. I cry out to You! I need You. I haven't clung to You like I should. Cause me to know Your loving-kindness in the morning. Thank You for sustaining me. Amen.

If you don't know the story of Joseph, detailed in the book of Genesis, it is wild. His brothers, who were jealous of his relationship with their father, sold him into slavery. As a captive, he had the opportunity to work for Potiphar, the captain of the Egyptian king's guard. But Joseph was set up by Potiphar's wife, whose seductive propositions he rejected, and he was sent to prison on false charges as a result.

And that's where things began to turn around for this guy. Behind bars, he had the opportunity to interpret the dream of the king's cupbearer and butler. Two years later, when the king had dreams he didn't understand, this cupbearer told him that Joseph was the man to help. And if you know the story, you know that not only did Joseph *help* the king, he was also released from prison and promoted to be the king's right-hand man.

What captures my imagination about Joseph's story is something we have very little information about, and that's the two-year stretch Joseph spent in prison *after* he'd helped the cupbearer. I'm curious if Joseph was just as faithful and hardworking as he'd been when he worked for Potiphar. We can look back at his childhood and see that he was a bit too sure of himself in some situations—sharing his dreams of grandeur with his brothers—and he needed to mature a little more. Were those years in prison the time when God worked on him, shaping him into the kind of man who could be second-in-command to Pharaoh?

Just as things were about to turn around for Joseph, the writer of Genesis announced, "Then it came to pass, at the end of two full years, that Pharaoh had a dream" (41:1). Joseph had spent years waiting, years in preparation. But when he was where he did not want to be, God was preparing him for the assignment that would ultimately impact countless lives—including the lives of his family members, and even more specifically, his brothers.

While I can only imagine what Joseph's prison season was like, I've certainly had seasons I wouldn't have chosen to endure—like when Lenya was sick and had so many needs, and I was getting such little sleep. In these times, we can ask God to give us His heart and *His* perspective on our situation. We can ask Him to help us see things the way He sees them. We can ask for His help to be faithful like Joseph in circumstances we didn't ask for or want at all.

INVITING THE LORD'S PRESENCE INTO THIS MOMENT

Every one of us has had a season we didn't ask for, one we never thought would or could happen. What are the challenges you are facing in this season? Take a moment to think of the specific ways God has prepared you for this. Consider what God might be doing or teaching you now that will be needed in a future season. Offer the Lord the challenges you're facing now. Let Jesus into the painful places. Open your heart to Him a little more, and lean into His mercies for today.

FRESH TRUST

He has made everything beautiful in its time. Also He has put eternity in their hearts, except that no one can find out the work that God does from beginning to end. I know that nothing is better for them than to rejoice, and to do good in their lives, and also that every man should eat and drink and enjoy the good of all his labor—it is the gift of God.

ECCLESIASTES 3:11–13

Lord God, I surrender my life to You. I can't see what You see, as You are outside of time, but I want to remember Your perspective, and I ask for glimpses of what You see. Teach me to trust in You in fresh ways, and to remember that my job is simply to rejoice in You and to do good with the life You have given me. Amen.

I WAS NINETEEN YEARS OLD, AND it felt like the whole world—including mine—was out of control. On this particular week, my mom was in the hospital having a C-section to deliver my twin sisters. And I knew my parents were struggling in their marriage. Four days later, I was scheduled to move to Albuquerque, New Mexico, for a yearlong internship. My heart ached, not knowing whether I should be leaving my family at such a critical time. In the midst of my inner turmoil—just three days before the twins were born—the World Trade Center was attacked and destroyed, and our country found itself plunged into a state of extreme grief and shock and pain. It did not seem like the time to pack up my silver 2000 Toyota Tacoma and drive two states away, leaving my family behind just as the world was seemingly falling apart. If even just one person had said, "You shouldn't go," I probably would have agreed and stayed.

As I look back at my journals from that time, I find it so comforting—and certainly *not* a coincidence—that the memory verse I'd been holding in my heart that week had led me so perfectly. In the midst of my chaos and

confusion, a passage from Ecclesiastes reminded me that, while I didn't understand God's plans, He could be trusted—fully.

These words sustained me during that week: "He has made everything beautiful in its time. Also He has put eternity in their hearts, except that no one can find out the work that God does from beginning to end. I know that nothing is better for them than to rejoice, and to do good in their lives" (Ecclesiastes 3:11–12).

At just the right time, God was teaching me that He makes everything beautiful in His time. And His time usually means it's not my time. *He* leads *me*. And that could honestly be the end of it, because if He is my Shepherd, then I have everything I need. But He doesn't just lead His sheep by the still waters or the green pastures; He also leads them through the valley of the shadow of death. Well, *that* doesn't feel very comforting or comfortable. But the most important thing is that He still is the One leading.

He knows the right time—because He is outside of it. When it feels like the timing isn't right, but it seems like He's leading, I can trust Him. I can lie down and rest. And this is exactly how the Lord was leading me in this period of my life. I knew God was leading me into the unknown experiences in New Mexico, but it was really painful to feel like I was walking out on my family, especially my mom and siblings, whom I felt needed me the most.

With tears streaming down my face, and watching my mother's tears fall, I kissed my twin baby sisters, hugged my other siblings, walked out of the hospital room, and drove away. I had to trust that God had my family, and that God was leading me into my future. It was all unknown and scary. But what I did know was that God was with me, and His timing was perfect—even though it didn't feel that way at the time.

INVITING THE LORD'S PRESENCE INTO THIS MOMENT

Make some space today to be still before the Lord. Take a few breaths and consider the fact that He is outside of time. He sees the end from the beginning. Rest in this.

What time frame are you in right now that might feel like the clock is going too slow or too fast, or possibly like it's not working at all? You're waiting on His timing, but it doesn't seem like He's even in the same time zone as you. Or maybe what He's asking of you doesn't make any sense. Ask Him to lead you in paths of righteousness for His name's sake. Tell Him what you're feeling and thinking. Renew your trust in Him. Tell Him you choose Him and His ways, even though you don't understand. And let God strengthen your faith and your trust in Him.

P.S.

As time went on (and as I met my future husband in the very place I was afraid to go), this verse in Ecclesiastes became an anthem for me personally, but it also became really special to Levi and me. It was the scripture we put on our wedding invitation, and it held us through our engagement as well as our marriage. And even after Lenya went to heaven, God brought such comfort to our hearts by reminding us of this verse and the truth that He has indeed set eternity in our hearts.

STRUGGLING WITH REGRET

The LORD is near to those who have a broken heart,
And saves such as have a contrite spirit.
Many are the afflictions of the righteous,
But the LORD delivers him out of them all.

PSALM 34:18–19

Thank You for being my God, who knows everything and is above it all. You see the beginning from the end, and I choose today to trust You. I do trust You. I don't understand, and I sometimes wish things were different, but I trust You. Thank You for being near to me, and thank You for Your comfort and peace and strength. You are my hope. Amen.

MY HEART WAS BROKEN. IT was the Valentine's Day after Lenya had gone to heaven. And while I knew that God was near to me, and I knew that Lenya was in His presence, my heart still ached. I wanted her in my arms. I wanted to hear her and Liv playing and laughing and even fighting.

I had so many moments of regret in those days following Lenya's death. It was suffocating at times, and I had to force myself to breathe deep and consider whose I was, not what I had done and how I had failed. My husband encouraged me to take it to God no matter how unpresentable it felt, reminding me that God was big enough to handle whatever I brought to Him. So, knowing that God was the only One who could comfort me, I turned to Him and to His Word.

Pouring my heart out to God, I confessed the regrets I had about the ways I had parented our sweet (and stubborn) girl. When I was too harsh.

Or impatient. When I had missed an important moment, or when I felt like I could have loved her better than I did. I just wanted the opportunity to love her even better and grow in my parenting of her. And I hated that I wouldn't have that chance, ever again, on this earth.

In His gentle way, God reminded me of His love for me. I resisted, protesting that I wasn't worthy. But God insisted, *My love is perfect and unconditional. It's not based on what you do or don't do. Rest in My love.*

IN HIS GENTLE WAY, GOD REMINDED ME OF HIS LOVE FOR ME.

Since that first Valentine's Day after Lenya died, I have seen so much growth in how I'm embracing this love from the Lord. I've also seen so much growth in my parenting. But I do still wish I'd been able to grow alongside Lenya. And when I have these moments of regret, these moments of longing, I continually give them back to the Lord. I don't understand, and I wish I could, but as I keep looking to Him, His perspective deepens in me and keeps me moving forward toward heaven in the way of life He designed for each of us to live.

INVITING THE LORD'S PRESENCE INTO THIS MOMENT

God is near to the brokenhearted. Where are you right now on the brokenhearted scale? Consider the nearness and love of your Father in heaven. Surrender to Him again whatever is breaking your heart. Hand over any regret you might feel. Melt into His strong, capable, loving arms. Ask Him to not only mend what has been broken but make it even stronger than before. It's what He does; it's who He is.

BE THE ANSWER TO YOUR OWN PRAYERS

Let Your work [the signs of Your power] be revealed to Your servants and Your [glorious] majesty to their children. And let the [gracious] favor of the Lord our God be on us; Confirm for us the work of our hands—Yes, confirm the work of our hands.

PSALM 90:16–17 AMP

My family and I were traveling home from a whip of a trip! For my husband's most recent book, *Blessed Are the Spiraling*, we went on a little sprint of a book tour—seven cities in seven days, starting in Dallas and ending in New York City. Each day we had a book signing and then a group run club; we called it the Spiraling Up Run Club Book Tour. It was incredible and so fun getting to meet people, hear their stories, and then run/walk together. (I was more in the walking category, FYI!)

Travel is a privilege and a gift, and I'm so thankful for it! But there is also the low side of it: delays, long travel days, whining, and crying (and that's just me, not to mention my kids). The final stretch on the way home can be the hardest part, because I'm ready to *just be home*. To be in my own bed. To get back into our home rhythm.

On this particular day, it was late. Our whole family was in the very back of the plane, and we knew our layover was not nearly long enough to get from plane A to plane B. As this plane landed, our next plane would be beginning to board. As we landed and then taxied to the gate, the flight attendant announced there were quite a few passengers who needed to get off the plane first in order to catch their connecting flights. We were hoping the sea of people would part, and we would glide down the aisle and make it without having to sprint through the airport to the next gate.

When the chime went off indicating that people could start getting their stuff and leave the plane, it was as if the entire crowd of passengers on the plane stood up, not considering the people in the back who really needed to get off the plane first.

I realized this was an issue, and so I started praying pretty intensely. (Although to God it probably sounded like a whining child.)

God, we're exhausted, we've been away from home for ten days, we've been everywhere, and we just want to be home! Lord, please hold the next plane! For whatever reason, hold that plane until we can get there! We don't want to spend the night in Salt Lake City—we want to be home!

I was praying like I'd never prayed before, but simultaneously it was looking like we weren't going to make it. There were twenty gates between our arrival and departure gates. I was well on the way to losing hope, but I also still believed at the same time.

Levi, Clover, and Daisy immediately started running once we were off the plane. Lennox and I started running as well, but we quickly lost steam. Bags in hand, backpacks on, it was a struggle just to keep moving. (Remember, I was part of the *walking* club, not the running club.)

As we neared the gate, I saw the agent standing there looking at us, her arms folded. We ran the last few yards, but Levi was standing there, and he said between gasps, "They barely held the plane for you!" I fully believe that if I hadn't had Lennox with me, the agent would have closed the door and left me behind. I think she had some grace for a little boy struggling to run toward the gate.

We walked down the aisle, avoiding any and all eye contact with any other passengers on the plane, and we found our seats as quickly as possible. We'd made it! Thank You, Jesus!

I sat down, breathing heavily (even though I hadn't run that hard) and thanking God for holding the plane for us. *He'd held the plane for us!*

Then I began to realize that the plane had *literally* been holding *for us*! *We* were the reason they'd held the plane. They'd been waiting for Lennox and me to get to the gate and get on the plane before they took off.

Wow. I was the answer to my own prayer! I had asked for God to hold the plane for us—for whatever reason—and the plane literally was held for *us*.

Sometimes God gives us the desires of our heart through ourselves, and it can change the way we run to God in prayer. *Lord, move in power in the way only You can! Let Your favor be on us, and help us! And Lord, if You choose to, do it through me!*

As we end this time we've spent together each day, I want to encourage you to pray bold prayers. And then ask God for the strength and bravery to be the answer to your own prayers. To walk by faith. To see each day as a fresh start, a fresh opportunity to be used by Him like never before.

Living the flourishing life we were meant to live begins with dependence on God in every moment. It starts with seeing His fresh mercies as a gift and as the launchpad into all He has for us in each moment.

A FINAL NOTE FROM THE AUTHOR

MERCY IN MOTION

Surely goodness and mercy shall follow me
All the days of my life;
And I will dwell in the house of the LORD
Forever.

PSALM 23:6

IT'S A BEAUTIFUL THING TO think about living every day awash in His goodness, His fresh mercies, and His compassion that never fails, and to think of how this will lead us to the ultimate day when we are in heaven with Jesus. I love this idea of mercy in motion. As we let Jesus be our Shepherd and lead us, goodness and mercy will follow us all the days of our lives. *Mercy will follow us*. There will be a motion of mercy every day of our lives.

But I wonder if this mercy is actually following us or if we're leaving it in our tracks wherever we go because we are following our loving and merciful God. His traits are becoming our traits, and we're leaving a trail of who He is so others can see and follow and know God as their Shepherd too.

I don't know a lot, but I do know that I want to follow my Good Shepherd. I know He has good plans for me as I choose to walk with Him, and they include receiving His fresh mercies every day—and that's my prayer for you too.

Acknowledgments

I am so grateful that my parents gave me my first diary on my eighth birthday, and that it launched me into a lifetime of writing and journaling. The practice of writing out my thoughts and prayers has truly helped me and given me handles in my walk with Jesus and in processing my own thoughts and griefs and joys. So thank you, Mom and Dad.

I am thankful for my husband, who pushes me to do the things I wouldn't do if I were left to myself. He speaks life over me. He tells me it's going to be okay, and that means everything. I love you, Levi. Thank you.

I am thankful for my kids, who have become such incredible cheerleaders and encouragers in my life—through all the prayers, the hugs, the notes, the words, the celebrations, and the laughter.

Thank you, Alivia, Daisy, Clover, Lennox, and Lenya; I am floored that I get to be your mom.

Thank you, Esther, for making things happen and for your encouragement. You're good at pouring fuel on dreams.

As I said at the start of this book, Jenn Dillon is a precious gem. She has allowed God to work deeply in her soul in the midst of heartache and grief, and the way she pours into her garden and creativity and art is a small glimpse into how she pours into her life—into her marriage and children and friendships and ministry. Thank you, Jenn, for being willing to partner with me, and for your courage and grace; it strengthens me all the time.

Thank you, Bonnie, for working your magic, and to Stephanie for keeping me on target.

Thank you, amazing Gift book team! Each of you made my dreams of a beautiful coffee table book devotional come true!

Thank you, Elisha Lynn and Katelyn, for your expertise and creativity, and for being the dynamic delightful duo.

Thank you, Nat, for your beautiful handwriting.

Hey, Fresh Life Church, I can't believe we get to love and serve God together! What God is doing in our midst is remarkable, and I love our staff, our impact team, and our whole church. Let's keep reaching the world together! Let's keep stretching!

About the Author

Jennie Lusko is a California girl who fell in love with a Colorado boy in New Mexico. They love Jesus and just want to live their lives for Him. Jennie and her husband, Levi, moved to Montana to start Fresh Life Church. It is the joy of their lives to serve God within the local church as well as the global church. Jennie and Levi have five kids who are lovely and who are changing the world: Alivia, Daisy, Clover, and Lennox—and Lenya, who is waiting for them in heaven. The Luskos make their home in Montana, until heaven!